THE FOOD-MOOD CONNECTION

Eating Your Way to Happiness

THE FOOD-MOOD CONNECTION
Eating Your Way to Happiness

Larry B. Christensen, Ph.D.

PRO-HEALTH PUBLICATIONS
P. O. Box 682
College Station, TX 77841

ISBN 0-9626509-7-8

LCCN 90-062144

First printing December 1990
Second printing June 1991

ATTENTION: MEDICAL PROFESSIONALS, CORPORATIONS, UNIVERSITIES, AND ASSOCIATIONS... Quantity discounts are available on bulk purchases of this book for educational purposes, sales premiums, or fund raising. Special books or book excerpts can also be created to fit specific needs. For information, please contact our Special Sales Department, Pro-Health Publications, P. O. Box 682, College Station, TX 77841.

Dedication

To My Wife Barbara

Acknowledgments

I want to give my sincere thanks to my wife Barbara for encouraging me to investigate the diet-behavior relationship. Without her encouragement I would probably still be a social psychologist and missed the opportunity to conduct some of the most exciting and useful research I have never encountered. It has made my life richer and more meaningful.

It would have been impossible to write this book without the patience and tolerance of the people who participated in my research studies. These individuals tolerated my initial failures as well as the rather significant demands the research placed on them to document each phase of the intervention process. Their patience and compliance has allowed me to uncover a simple procedure that can help numerous individuals overcome depression.

Special thanks go to my children, Tanya and Troy, my brother, Dr. Andrew Christensen, Jr., my sister, Jan LaBarbara, and Jennifer Kohl for reading parts or all of the manuscript and giving me their valuable input. Their comments not only improved the accuracy of the manuscript, but also improved the overall quality of the book.

Finally, I would like to thank Marilyn Ross for her editorial savvy. Without her input the book would have been far too academic and the readability would have been compromised.

All opinions, facts, and judgments are exclusively my own.

About the Author

 **Dr. Larry Christensen** has been an academic psychologist conducting research and writing for numerous professional journals for over 23 years. Now a professor and Director of Graduate Studies in the psychology branch of Texas A&M University, Dr. Christensen has also been a research consultant to the Texas Department of Mental Health.

He has served as president of the Southwestern Psychological Association as well as being a member of the American Psychological Association and the Society for the Psychological Study of Social Issues.

Once happily teaching and doing social psychological research, Dr. Christensen discovered the food-mood connection through events which altered his professional career—and the lives of countless people. Intrigued by books lent by a woman struggling with depression and using diet to fight it off, the author committed to in-depth research. That investigation lasted over a decade and culminates in the sound strategy of *The Food-Mood Connection*. Subjected to the rigorous standards of his tests, Dr. Christensen's results come to light in this encompassing book.

Table of Contents

PART I

DIET THERAPY
WHAT IT IS
AND
HOW TO APPLY IT

CHAPTER 1

Are You a Dietary Responder?

Have you ever felt tired and worn out even though you've been getting enough sleep? Ever felt so down in the dumps you didn't care about anything? Or perhaps you've felt bad and couldn't figure out why. Have you ever had a feeling of internal nervousness or inner trembling for no apparent reason? Are you moody and find you have outbursts of anger you have no control over? Do you have difficulty sleeping? Have you made an appointment with your family physician to find out what was wrong with you—only to be told you were perfectly healthy?

If you are one of those people who suffers from several or all of these problems, I can empathize with you. You're not alone. There are a lot of people who feel the same way. Some have even decided there is no help; that this is just the way they are and they must accept and live with it. But, what you want is relief from your symptoms. You want to feel good!

Now I want to do something that might sound strange. I want to congratulate you! Why? Because you've chosen to read this book. In doing so you may have taken the first step toward feeling good and getting rid of all those symptoms that constantly make you so run down and miserable.

In the following chapters you'll discover how you may be able to overcome these problems by avoiding a few foods. As a research scientist, I became interested in the connection between food and mood over a decade ago. We're often told all we have to do to get well and feel better is to take vitamins, eat natural foods, exercise, or follow some combination of these suggestions. If this were correct, we would have wiped out virtually all physical and psychological problems. While vitamins, natural foods, and exercise are important and necessary, they don't solve all problems—particularly those discussed in this book.

The book you are reading is the outgrowth of many years of research conducted on people just like yourself. Most of the individuals participating in my studies were recruited from advertisements such as the following:

Depressed, Moody, Feeling Tired, Sad, or Blue?

The Department of Psychology is conducting a study of the cause and treatment of individuals who are depressed, often feel tired even though they sleep a lot, suffer from headaches, or are very moody and generally seem to feel bad and unhappy most of the time. If you have one or more of these symptoms and would like to participate in the study please contact...

Would you have answered this advertisement? Fortunately, many people did. From such participation I have been able to identify those individuals that will respond to dietary intervention. I've also been able to identify the foods that can cause symptoms such as depression, fatigue, mental confusion, and moodiness.

Before going any further I want to correct a misconception I may be giving you. I have not identified the cure for cases of depression, fatigue, and mental confusion. These symptoms can be caused by many different things.

For example, my wife told me about a woman she knew who hung herself. This woman had a stroke several years ago that caused brain damage. Whenever she took an antibiotic for an infection she became severely depressed. Her friends and family knew this and would watch her closely whenever she was on antibiotics. On the fatal evening she apparently awoke in the middle of the night, walked into the garage and hung herself. Her husband woke up at about 4 A.M. and, not finding his wife next to him, jumped out of bed and began searching for her. He looked in every room of the house and finally opened the door into the garage. There he found his wife hanging from the rafters. A sad but true story.

I knew a man whose wife had divorced him. Shortly after the divorce he lost his job and was forced to accept welfare. This individual felt that life was meaningless. He was having difficulty sleeping, lost his appetite, and was very pessimistic about things getting any better.

Recently, the *APA Monitor*, the official newsletter of the American Psychological Association, had a special article on environmental toxins. The dramatic effect environmental toxins can have on our physical and mental health was illustrated by the case of a woman who had worked for Lockheed, an airplane manufacturing company, for 9½ years. During this time her physical appearance changed considerably. She constantly wore gloves because of severe skin and nail problems. She wore dark glasses even indoors because her eyes couldn't tolerate light. Mentally she was a wreck. Her memory was shot, she cried a lot, and had piercing headaches for which she received demerol shots, to relieve the pain. She also screamed at people who didn't deserve it and frequently had thoughts of suicide.

These are three instances of depression which are clearly not caused by diet. In the first example, the depression was clearly organic. Apparently the stroke the woman had several years earlier altered her brain chemistry in such a way that antibiotics would trigger a depressive episode. In the second example, the divorce and job loss appeared to cause the depression. The physical and psychological problems in the third example stemmed from the toxic chemicals the woman was exposed to at work. She was exposed to drums containing chemicals that weren't sealed correctly, as well as chemicals that had splattered on the floor.

Problems such as these are obviously not due to food. It is necessary to differentiate such cases from those related to food. In later chapters of this book I will give you some guidelines you can follow to help determine if your problem is food related or not. In addition to using these guidelines you should also see your physician to determine if your problem may be caused by something other than food.

The important point is some problems are food related; others are not. If yours happens to be food related, you're fortunate. You can control the way you feel simply by altering your eating patterns! If you want to feel good and have energy you must eat one way. If you violate the rules and eat the things that will make you feel ill, so be it. You can eat them and suffer the consequences. The good news is you have total control over this aspect of your well being.

CHAPTER 2

Depression—Potentially Deadly and Often Not Treated

Bill Black was a successful 35-year-old lawyer with a beautiful wife and two teenagers. On the surface he represented the epitome of success. He had a booming practice that provided sufficient income to allow him and his family to take several vacations a year, and enjoy skiing in the winter and scuba diving in the summer. Three years ago Bill started having difficulty sleeping. He would go to bed and lie there for what seemed like hours before going to sleep. When he did finally doze off it was often a fitful sleep. He would wake up feeling just as tired as when he went to bed. At other times Bill would awake at 3:00 or 4:00 in the morning, unable to get back to sleep. Or, if sleep did come, it seemed like it was only in 15 or 20 minute segments.

Bill went to his family physician who prescribed sleeping pills. These helped some. However, they did not give him the quality of sleep he desired; if he took too many he felt like he had a hangover the next morning. As time went by, the sleep problem worsened, and other symptoms developed. Bill began losing his appetite. Food just did not taste good and he began to lose weight.

Bill's wife began to notice he was not his normal happy self. While he had previously been a good lover, Bill was making fewer and fewer advances. This bothered her. She wondered if she was loosing her sex appeal. To bolster Bill's interest she bought the slinkiest, sexiest negligee she could find: hoping to kindle the sexual, romantic yearnings she and Bill had experienced so many times during their 10 years of marriage. This time Bill was not responsive. Not only did he not respond to his wife's advance, he had no interest in sex.

Bill's wife was not only concerned about his lack of interest in virtually anything, she was also getting fed up with what seemed to be his increasing laziness. Bill had always been physically active. The last several years he seemed to be laying around the house more and more. He began complaining of constant fatigue, saying he was always tired regardless of how much sleep he got. It didn't matter how much Bill's wife did for him or how long he slept, he never felt good and never felt like doing anything anymore. Bill's friends quit calling him because he always made excuses for not joining in their traditional Saturday golf game, or even a Friday after-work drink.

Not only did Bill develop a number of physical complaints, but his behavior and sense of self worth were at an all time low. Although Bill was a very successful lawyer he didn't feel like it. He felt like a total failure as a lawyer, father, husband, and lover. He felt his life was a total sham. No matter what he did or how much apparent success he had, he received no joy or pleasure from it. Instead, he increasingly felt guilty and worthless and that life was not worth living. "What's the point of continuing?" he asked.

How Prevalent Is Depression?

Bill was experiencing a severe case of depression. His whole life was disrupted. Not only was he miserable, but he was making life miserable for his entire family. Unfortunately, the misery experienced by Bill and his family is also experienced by millions of others and their loved ones. A recent study published in the *Archives of General Psychiatry* estimated that, at any one point in time, at least 10-14 million Americans are afflicted by some form of depression severe enough to need treatment. Studies such as this also reveal as many as one in every ten Americans may experience a severe mood disturbance at some time in their life. The World Health Organization has estimated that, each year, approximately 100 million people world-wide experience depression. As you can see, this is a wide-spread phenomenon common to virtually all cultures. In fact, it is so common some individuals consider it to be the *common cold of psychiatric disorders*.

You might think that people with a disorder this common would seek and get appropriate treatment. Unfortunately, this is not the case. For example, one of the individuals I treated with the dietary intervention I will discuss later in this book was a 54-year-old woman. She had lived with her depression for over 20 years! She thought it was something she had to accept and live with the rest of her life. This is not an unusual case. Many depressed people either don't get treatment or get inappropriate treatment.

Depression Can Kill You

The sad part is depression can kill you. Most people either don't realize this or think something like this could not happen to them or one of their family members. Often they think the person is *too sensible to do anything as stupid as kill themselves*. Depressed people, however, tend to view life as not worth living and often feel as though they would be better off dead. They may even think their family and friends would be better off if they were dead.

Some depressed individuals actually do commit suicide. Studies of suicide rates reveal depressed patients are 100 to 500 times more likely to kill themselves than are the nondepressed. Of all those who commit suicide, 45 to 70 percent are suffering from depression. Most of these people have received absolutely no help for their problem.

Most Depressed People
Do Not Get the Right Treatment

Studies have revealed that only about 20 percent of individuals with an emotional problem seek help from a mental health professional, the most appropriate person to assist them. Instead of going to a mental health professional, these individuals typically make an appointment with their family physician. In doing so, they may not get the type of help they need.

Why would a depressed person do this rather than seek a mental health professional who could treat them more effectively? The main reason is they inappropriately label their symptoms. Look at what Bill was experiencing. He couldn't sleep, his appetite was poor, he was not interested in sex, and he was constantly tired. Most people with these symptoms would think they have a physical, rather than a mental disorder—and make an appointment with their family physician. People with emotional disorders such as depression have these types of symptoms in addition to psychological symptoms such as feelings of worthlessness. If you go back and read Bill's story again, you will see that in addition to not being able to sleep and having a poor appetite, he had a low self image and felt worthless. Most people do not connect the physical symptoms with these subjective psychological symptoms. Yet in depression and other mood disturbances they are connected. Unless these two sets of symptoms are linked, a person will tend to seek relief for the physical symptoms first. This typically means contacting a physician.

When a despondent person contacts his or her family physician about problems with one of the symptoms of depression, such as the inability to sleep or constant fatigue, the doctor usually searches for a cause of just this disorder. If inability to fall asleep is the most dominant problem, and this is what a patient complains about, then the physician will undoubtedly prescribe sleeping pills. In this way only one of the symptoms of depression is treated. If constant fatigue is the problem, the doctor may request a thyroid function test. If the thyroid gland is not producing an adequate supply of the hormone thyroxine, a person will feel very tired. The point is, the physician must question patients not only about the problems they present—but also about other symptoms they may have in order to uncover the depression. If this is not done, the doctor will treat only one of the symptoms of depression, and not the depression itself. In order to uncover the depression, the physician must know its symptoms and question the patient about other complaints as well as those that are mentioned. Unfortunately, this extensive probing does not often exist.

So far a gloomy picture has been presented. Depression is a serious and potentially deadly disorder that afflicts many Americans. Most of them get inappropriate treatment. The good news is there are attempts to educate the public so they will correctly identify their symptoms as depression and get the right treatment.

How Depression Is Treated

Drug Therapy

The most common treatment of depression, and the one most people seek, is drug therapy. There are many effective antidepressant drugs on the market which go by the names of Adapin, Amitril, Asendin, Deprol, Desyrel, Elavil, Endep, Etrafon, Limbitrol, Ludiomil, Marplan, Nardil, Norpramin, Pamelor, Parnate, Pertofrane, Prozac, Sinequan, Surmontil, Tofranil, Triavil and Vivactil.

Do these drugs work? Definitely. But not for everyone. Most people who take them pay a price—and I don't mean money. These drugs produce a number of possible side effects such as loss of energy, fatigue, agitation, increased sweating, dry mouth, constipation, water retention, blurred vision, aggravation of glaucoma, confusion, weight gain, altered sexual drive, and even seizures in extreme cases.

Most people taking antidepressant medication experience only a few of these side effects. Fatigue, loss of energy, dry mouth, and constipation are quite common. In some individuals these side effects are so intense they quit taking the medication. For them, the *cure* is worse than the disease.

One individual I treated with the dietary intervention had been taking Desyrel for some time. Her primary complaint was not that it wasn't doing any good, but that it made her hair dry and she always had such a dry mouth. It was so unpleasant she was willing to try anything else that would allow her to stop taking Desyrel. In addition to such side effects, many of the antidepressant drugs take from two to four weeks to have any effect. Doctors don't know which antidepressant drug will work best for a particular patient. This means you have to try one. If it works, that's great—especially if you're one of those people who have few side effects, but if the drug doesn't work, then you have to try another—and then another—until the one with the best antidepressant effects and the least side effects is found. This process could take months before a solution is found.

Psychotherapy

In addition to drug therapy, research has revealed several types of psychotherapy that can effectively treat depression. Interpersonal Psychotherapy and Cognitive Therapy are the two most popular forms. Interpersonal Psychotherapy evolved from the 10 years of experience the New Haven-Boston Collaborative Depression Project gained from treating and doing research with depressed patients. Interpersonal Psychotherapy assumes that depression occurs because of difficulties we have with other people. These difficulties could involve dealing with the death of a loved one, problems with a marriage, losing a job, or coping with a divorce. Therapy involves defining the problem area or areas causing the depression. Strategies are then developed for treating the depression. If you feel depressed because a good friend died, therapy may consist of having you think about the loss to speed up the grieving process and, at the same time, help you establish new friends that can substitute for the one you lost.

Cognitive Therapy, developed by Dr. Aaron Beck and his colleagues at the University of Pennsylvania School of

Medicine makes the assumption that all of our moods, including depression, are created by our thoughts. If you feel good, it is because you are having happy, pleasant thoughts. If you're down in the dumps it is because you are having negative thoughts. This idea that our thought patterns control our emotions has some validity. For example, if you are thinking about the fun you will have on your vacation, or about your boyfriend or lover coming home on the weekend, you will probably be happy and feel good. On the other hand, if you start thinking about the car trouble you're having, or a friend who is saying unpleasant things about you, then you will probably start feeling low. Cognitive Therapy assumes that depression develops as a result of having negative thoughts. To eliminate depression you must reorient your thought patterns from negative to positive.

The National Institute of Mental Health just completed a 5-million-dollar study investigating the effectiveness of both of these forms of psychotherapy as well as drug therapy. The study confirmed what other studies had also demonstrated. Both of these forms of psychotherapy are as effective as drug therapy. However, both Interpersonal Psychotherapy and Cognitive Therapy have their limitations. They cannot effectively treat everyone. No single therapy can. Not even drug therapy. In fact, the National Institute of Mental Health study revealed that each of these three therapies was effective in eliminating the depression of only 50 to 60 percent of the individuals they treated. This means that other approaches must be identified for treating depression. The dietary approach I have developed is one of these alternative approaches.

Interpersonal Psychotherapy and Cognitive Therapy are also promoted as short term remedies. They are short term, however, only with respect to therapies such as Psychoanalytic Therapy, the type developed by Sigmund Freud. A person can be in Psychoanalytic Therapy for years. Interpersonal Psychotherapy and Cognitive Therapy typically takes only 8 to 12 weeks of treatment. While this is much shorter than psychoanalysis, it would be nice if depression could be treated quicker. *And it can.* I have developed a dietary treatment program that will work within one to three weeks if you stick to it religiously. That is much shorter than the 8 to 12 weeks required for psychotherapy and my method doesn't have side effects like drug therapy has.

Dietary Therapy

The dietary therapy presented in this book is a revolution in the treatment of mood disorders. It gets at the *cause* of the depression and is something you can do by yourself and have total control over. With the dietary approach you no longer have to rely on a psychiatrist for medication or a Cognitive Therapist to help you reorient your thoughts. All you have to do is eliminate certain foods from your diet.

By now I'm sure you're thinking, "Is this guy crazy? Does he really think that I can eliminate my feelings of worthlessness, my fatigue, and my despair by simply cutting out certain foods?" If these are your thoughts let me assure you that I've had some of the same thoughts during the many years I have been researching this topic. Several of my students and clients have also had these thoughts. One of them felt that a *dumb old diet* couldn't help her. However, she was desperate—and nothing else she had tried had helped her—so she tried the dietary intervention on the outside chance it might do some good. Much to her surprise, she started feeling less depressed in four days. Within only a week she was beginning to be her normal self.

A clinical psychology graduate student recently told one of my students, Ros Burrows, that the client Ros was working with was so depressed that diet couldn't possibly help her. Ros calmly told the clinical psychology graduate student that all of the tests he had given his client indicated the diet would help and that if it did not he would refer her back to the Psychology Clinic for traditional psychotherapy. After two weeks had elapsed the clinical graduate student approached Ros and asked him when he was going to refer the client back to the clinic so she could administer psychotherapy to her. Ros replied, "I don't think you want her now. The diet eliminated most of her depression." The graduate student gave a surprised, "Oh," and walked off. Such expressions of surprise are common because the dietary therapy is new and totally inconsistent with traditional thought regarding the causes of depression. However, it works. And the exciting thing about it is it is a very simple type of treatment.

CHAPTER 3

How I Became Interested in Diet and Behavior

About 15 years ago I was a content academic psychologist teaching and conducting social psychological research at Texas A&M University. It was at about this time that a set of events began which eventually altered my professional career and the lives of countless people.

Beth, an attractive school teacher I knew, had always been slightly moody. It was nothing major and didn't interfer with her social, personal, or professional life. But the tendency was there.

Beth's problems seemed to begin when her energy level started declining. She just didn't have the energy she would like to have and this interfered with her lifestyle. She became fatigued easily and didn't have the stamina to teach, maintain her household, and provide care for her two small children. As the fatigue and her concern over it increased, Beth did what most people would do. She made an appointment with her physician. He checked her for hypothyroidism. The test found that her thyroid level was very low so he placed her on synthetic thyroid. The results were good. In several months her energy level returned and she was back on course.

Over a period of several years, however, Beth's energy level again began to decline. Her physician scheduled her for another thyroid function test. This time the test was normal, but Beth still felt fatigued. It was not a constant fatigue but one that would engulf her at unpredictable and unexpected times. She could be teaching or walking from one room to another in the house and suddenly be engulfed with fatigue. It was as though her energy was suddenly being drained out of her.

It was at about this time that one of Beth's friends told her about the benefit of protein in restoring energy and about a source of protein wafers. She tried them and found they helped. She bought large quantities so she could take them to work and munch on them throughout the day. When Beth informed me of their benefit, I scoffed at the idea. How could munching on a protein wafer increase your energy level? Beth even encouraged me to try them, which I did. They had no effect on my energy level and did absolutely nothing for me. (Little did I know I would eventually become a believer and that research would verify such a relationship exists in some individuals.)

Beth's concern with her energy level was soon overshadowed by severe and sharp pains in her back and down her arm. Her symptoms were classic and indicated a gallbladder problem. Beth was scheduled for a gallbladder X-ray that week. But the X-ray did not reveal any gallstones; it actually showed her gallbladder was in good shape. Beth was somewhat distressed over this news. But the pain disappeared so she soon forgot about it.

Beth remained free of pain for about a year and then she had another attack. This led to another X-ray that again revealed nothing. The attacks continued, however, becoming increasingly more frequent and severe. Beth made an appointment with another physician to get a second opinion. This second physician scheduled yet another X-ray with the same perplexing results — everything was in good shape.

Beth battled this gallbladder agony for several years, enduring the pain, numerous laboratory tests, and various diets and treatments from several physicians—all with no beneficial results. The pain continued. Nothing anyone did provided relief. Finally all attempts to eliminate the pain had been tried and the only option left was exploratory surgery.

The surgery revealed Beth had a diseased, inflamed gallbladder. No gallstones were present. The surgeon informed her that this happens in about 5 percent of the cases and an X-ray cannot detect this diseased condition. Finally, after several years of pain the cause had been found and the gallbladder removed. Beth anticipated recovery and returning to a normal life.

Although she recovered from the surgery, her energy level did not return. In fact, it got worse and she began to develop other symptoms such as mental confusion, depression, and sleep difficulties. Beth's physician could find nothing physically wrong with her. He suggested the symptoms were probably due to the stress of her job so she quit teaching. The symptoms did not disappear; Instead they got worse.

Beth's physician could not find anything physically that might be responsible for her symptoms, so he suggested that the cause might be psychological. Beth bristled at the thought. She knew what a psychological problem was like and these symptoms were not psychological. However, she agreed to have a psychological evaluation. It was inconclusive. There did not seem to be a good psychological explanation for her symptoms either.

By this time Beth was searching for a solution on her own. This is when Beth began her journey into health food stores and began to read books pertaining to hypoglycemia. The symptoms described in these books fit her perfectly. She went back to her physician and asked him about the possibility that she was hypoglycemic. He dismissed the idea.

Undaunted, Beth decided to follow the advise presented in the books she was reading. To her delight she began to see some improvement. It was about this time that Beth began to encourage me to look at the books she was reading. At first I resisted, but I finally agreed.

The books I read were fascinating. The authors were good journalists and wrote a fascinating account of how altering one's diet can eliminate all kinds of physical and psychological problems. According to these authors, diet was the key to curing virtually all the sins of the world from diabetes to alcoholism. Obviously I didn't believe that diet could cure all physical and mental disorders. However, after reading several of these books I became convinced that there had to be an element of truth to what was being said. "There was too much smoke for there not to be some fire."

At this point I made a commitment to look into the concept. I knew that, if there was something to the accusations made by these authors, I had the necessary research skills to identify them. Also, if there was anything to the accusations it would represent a significant contribution to the field of psychology and to the whole mental health profession.

Now I needed to decide not only where to start but what to investigate. By this time I'd made contact with a physician who used the dietary approach in his practice. Dr. Mitchell was pleased to have another professional who did not scoff at his approach and constantly informed me of workshops being held which promoted various aspects of the dietary approach.

For the next year I tried to maintain an open mind and look at all the various techniques and information Dr. Mitchell and others fed me. I learned about reflexology and kinesiology. Reflexology is a technique that involves massaging various points on the foot to promote health. Kinesiology is a process whereby you are supposed to be able to diagnose the needs of a person by the strength of their arm. This process requires a person to hold a substance such as medication, vitamins, or minerals in their hand. They then hold their arm out to their side, parallel to the floor, and the kinesiologist presses down on the arm. When something is bad for an individual the arm weakens, when it is good for the individual it strengthens.

I even encountered a dentist who thought you could ask an individual questions and obtain the answers by the strength of their arm. He believed that the arm would weaken when a person was lying and would strengthen when the person was telling the truth.

Then Dr. Mitchell introduced me to a technique that made use of magnets. He told me about this wonderful workshop being held in Houston conducted by a chiropractor that I should attend. I finally agreed and paid my $75.00 admission fee. At this workshop I was told you could diagnose the needs of the body by having a person lie on their back and look at the length of their legs. Ideally a person's legs should be the same length and if they are not something is wrong in the body.

This chiropractor would place vitamins and minerals on a person's stomach, place a magnet over them, then check the length of the person's legs. When the length of the legs was identical that represented the right combination or amount of vitamins. We were given a demonstration using a cancer patient and, after using this method to diagnose this person's needs, the chiropractor emphatically stated the boy would be cured of his cancer if he would just take these vitamins and minerals.

The final technique Dr. Mitchell introduced me to was a variant of acupuncture. It was called electroacupuncture. At least this had an authentic ring to it. I knew research had been conducted on acupuncture and that it seemed to work. Dr. Mitchell had attended a workshop that taught him how to use a seemingly sophisticated machine to diagnose and treat various physical and mental problems.

This machine supposedly represented an advancement over the traditional acupuncture technique of inserting and twirling needles. A small electrical stimulation was applied at various acupuncture pressure points. This was supposed to be a superior substitute for the needles. Not only that, but it purported to contain a variety of other gadgets that allowed you to identify the medications and the amounts needed to treat an individual.

At this time I was still floundering around trying to decide how I was going to investigate the relationship between diet and behavior and exactly what I was going to investigate. A year had passed and I'd made no progress on the diet-behavior relation. Maybe I should rephrase that. I had made no visible progress. I knew of the fringe approaches that were being advocated and that all they were doing was giving general advice which had no scientific support. I wasn't about to begin using them or conduct any research on them. At the same time I had begun a rather significant literature review trying to identify information focusing on the relationship between behavior and diet. There is actually a large body of scientific literature, but it was not focused and did not give me any clues as to what to study or how to proceed with my investigation.

It was time to either identify a specific approach to take in investigating the behavior-diet relationship, or go back to being a social psychologist. I was still convinced that a relationship existed between behavior and diet so I decided to identify something specific to investigate. But what? Then I asked myself, "What is the common thread running through virtually all the various approaches and material I encountered?" The common thread seemed to be the underlying assumption that hypoglycemia was the cause of many physical and emotional disorders. Although I didn't believe this, I decided to investigate hypoglycemia—which means low blood sugar. Many symptoms such as fatigue are present when blood sugar levels are low. I needed to become acquainted with what was already known about this disorder. I spent months in the library reading virtually all the available scientific articles written on this subject. For the next several months I read over a 1,000 articles on hypoglycemia and went back to the original 1924 article by Seale Harris, who first identified the condition of hypoglycemia.

Much to my surprise, I found that hypoglycemia could mimic a variety of both physical and psychological disorders. There were instances of people with undiagnosed cases of hypoglycemia who had been treated for other disorders, such as schizophrenia. I also became aware that various professional organizations such as the American Medical Association were adamant about the fact that hypoglycemia was an infrequent disorder and that it did not account for many cases of misdiagnosis.

This actually is true. Hypoglycemia occurs quite infrequently. However, my review of the literature revealed that a good study had not been conducted which investigated the prevalence of hypoglycemia in a psychiatric population. I decided this was the most appropriate place for me to begin.

To conduct this research I decided I must use only individuals who were undergoing psychological counseling and who were also experiencing the symptoms of hypoglycemia. I constructed a checklist of all the symptoms expressed by people with hypoglycemia and had people seeking psychological counseling from the University Counseling Center complete the checklist. The following table presents a partial list of these symptoms, which illustrates the many and varied symptoms expressed by the hypoglycemic patient.

Those people who had many of the symptoms were considered good candidates for hypoglycemia and were requested to go to the University Medical Center for a 5-hour oral glucose tolerance test. This is the test that is used to diagnose hypoglycemia. Much to my chagrin, none of the these people showed up as having hypoglycemia. I asked over twenty people to take the oral glucose tolerance test and none of them were hypoglycemic.

This was not the right approach. Even though these people had hypoglycemic-type symptoms, they were not hypoglycemic and it was foolish to continue on this track.

A Partial List of Symptoms
Hypoglycemic Patients Experience

Apathy	Exhaustion	Muscle Pain
Blurred Vision	Fatigue	Negativism
Can't Tolerate Stress	Forgetfulness	Nervousness
Craving for Coffee	Hand Tremor	Poor Memory
Craving for Sweets	Headaches	Poor Judgement
Crying Easily	Internal Trembling	Restless Legs
Depression	Irritability	Sensitive to Light
Detached Feelings	Lack of Sex Drive	Short Temper
Difficulty in Speaking	Lack of Appetite	Suicidal Thoughts
Disorientation	Light-headed	Thirsty
Dizziness	Mental Confusion	Weakness
Dry Mouth	Moody	Worrying

The American Medical Association was right. Hypoglycemia seldom causes psychological problems. In fact, a case can be made for hypoglycemia not even being a disorder because everyone has low blood sugar from time to time and everyone does not experience the symptoms of hypoglycemia. However, that is another story.

At this point I was convinced I was not dealing with hypoglycemia and I didn't even want to talk about hypoglycemia. Now I was beginning to be depressed. I had spent several years looking into fringe techniques as well as the literature on hypoglycemia and my first study investigating the incidence of hypoglycemia in people with psychological problems was a bust.

Fortunately, a fortuitous event happened that gave me the encouragement I needed to keep going. I asked several of the people who took the test for hypoglycemia to try the diet I had prepared even though the oral glucose tolerance test indicated that they were not hypoglycemic. I had been optimistic about the possibility that some of the people with hypoglycemic symptoms would be hypoglycemic so I had prepared the standard high-protein and low-carbohydrate diet. I also made another fortuitous decision. I totally eliminated refined sugar and caffeine from this high-protein and low-carbohydrate diet.

Several people agreed to try the diet. Much to my surprise, they reported it made them feel better and eliminated many of their symptoms. This gave me that glimmer of hope that I needed. Maybe all my efforts were not in vain. Maybe I had made the correct decision to look into the relationship between behavior and diet. However, I also knew that I was still a long way from verifying this relationship and definitely a long way from convincing my colleagues that such a relationship existed.

CHAPTER 4

Development of the Dietary Treatment Program

My research on the relationship between diet and behavior had reached the point where I had evidence indicating that the dietary treatment might benefit some emotionally distressed individuals. Now I had to convince myself and then my colleagues that this was really true. The only way I could do this was to develop sound scientific data indicating that the diet, and only the diet, caused an improvement and elimination of symptoms.

The first step I took was more to convince myself than my colleagues. This step involved identifying individuals who might profit from the diet, have them record the number of symptoms they experienced each day for about two weeks, and then have them follow the dietary program I had prepared. I wanted to see how much the symptoms fluctuated naturally from day to day and then what happened when they started following the diet.

The key factor in the diet's success was selecting people who would profit from the diet. Who were these people and how did I identify them? The only procedure I had available was the checklist of hypoglycemic-like symptoms I had developed. Using it, I identified several individuals who stated they experienced many of the same symptoms as did a person with hypoglycemia.

One of the first individuals I identified kept a record of symptoms for nine days. Then she followed the high-protein, low-carbohydrate, caffeine and refined sucrose-free diet for eleven days. The results were amazing. Look at her data displayed in figure 4.1. She was experiencing 5 to 12 symptoms a day before the dietary intervention. Following the dietary intervention her symptoms disappeared with the exception of the day when she ate the cinnamon toast. I was elated. The diet works!

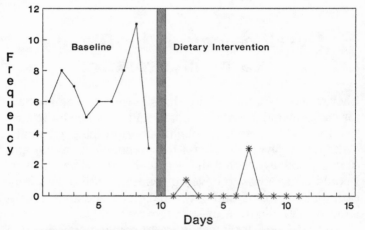

FIGURE 4.1 Frequency of symptoms experienced prior to and following dietary intervention

To further convince myself, I followed the same procedure with a male in his early twenties. This man kept a diary of the frequency of symptoms he was experiencing for 15 days and then followed the same high-protein, low-carbohydrate, caffeine and refined sucrose-free diet for the next month. During this time (see figure 4.2) his symptoms disappeared—unless he violated the dietary restrictions like the times when he increased his carbohydrate load, or drank a grape soda. He was elated with the results and so was I. Once again the dietary intervention had proven successful.

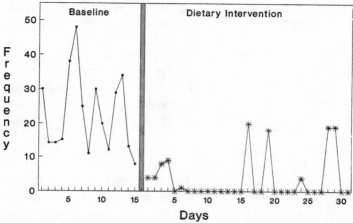

FIGURE 4.2 Frequency of symptoms experienced prior to and following dietary intervention

Although I was elated with the results, the data I had collected was not sufficient to convince my fellow scientists that the diet was effective. Look at figure 4.2. You can see the symptom frequency was not recorded for much of the time during which the diet was followed. When I inquired as to why the symptom frequency was not maintained this individual said he didn't think this was necessary because he was feeling good and was symptom free. Little did he know I needed the data to convince others that the diet works.

The research design I was using also provided inadequate proof of the effectiveness of the diet. The research design I used with these two individuals is called a single subject A-B time series design. It is a design that is used with one person. Data, such as the frequency with which symptoms are experienced each day, are collected on many different days before the treatment is administered (the A phase) and for many days after the treatment is administered (the B phase). The problem with this design is that factors other than the dietary intervention could also explain the results. The most obvious one is that the individuals knew that their diet was being changed and they may have expected some improvement. This is called an expectancy effect. When we expect something to happen we often inadvertently make it happen.

These expectations can be very powerful. It is like giving someone a sugar pill for an illness rather than the antibiotic they should be given. If they think they are receiving an antibiotic, even though they are really receiving the sugar pill, the sugar pill can actually make them feel better.

This expectancy effect was demonstrated most vividly in an experiment where angina sufferers, people with a spasmodic choking or suffocating pain, agreed to undergo either a heart bypass operation or merely simulate the bypass operation by having their chest opened and then closed. They were not told who would receive which operation.

The results were remarkable. The people who merely had their chest opened and the closed again but did not have a bypass experienced as much relief as did those who actually had the bypass operation. The only explanation for this effect was that everyone expected to feel better following the operation. Why else would they have gone through so much pain and suffering? This expectation worked even for those who had nothing done to them other than having their chest opened and closed again. It is this type of expectation that must be eliminated to convince my fellow scientists that the diet was effective.

How could I eliminate this possible expectancy effect and demonstrate that the results I was getting were due only to the diet? At this time I thought the symptom checklist I had developed was a decent tool for identifying the dietary responder or the individual who could profit from the dietary intervention. I thought all I needed to do to convince my colleagues was to identify a group of people experiencing many of the symptoms on the symptom checklist and then conduct an experiment that demonstrated when those individuals were given my dietary intervention they experienced a lessening of their symptoms and a reduction in their emotional distress—whereas people who were given some other diet to follow did not experience such benefits.

I actually conducted this experiment and it was a total flop. Not only was there no difference between the two groups in terms of the benefits they received from the two dietary treatments, but many of the people who were given the high-protein, low-carbohydrate, caffeine and refined sucrose-free diet did not experience an elimination in their symptoms.

All kinds of thoughts raced through my head. Was I wrong? Were the wonderful results I had previously obtained due just to expectancy and not the diet? Had I wasted several years of my professional career chasing rainbows? I had to do some heavy soul searching. The final factor convincing me there *was* an effect even though the experiment was a flop was that some of the people in the experiment did receive a tremendous benefit.

Why would some people benefit and not others? The only answer I could come up with was that the symptom checklist was not doing a good job of selecting the people who would respond to the dietary intervention. I then began a several year process of revising this checklist and developing it into a good psychological test that continues to be used in selecting the dietary sensitive individual.

At the same time as I was working on the development of this psychological test I also continued working on verifying the effectiveness of the dietary treatment. To do this I had to eliminate the possibility that the effect I was getting was due just to expectancy. The ideal situation for accomplishing this was to feed an individual a diet without their knowing what they were eating. The best way of doing this, at least that I knew of, was to insert a tube into their stomach and feed them through it. This was something I didn't have the ability or expertise to do. Therefore, I decided to take the next best option and go back to using a single subject type of design which does a decent job of eliminating rival hypotheses such as expectancies.

About this time I was asked to present a departmental colloquium explaining the results of my labors. I eagerly agreed to do so and talked for about an hour about my research, outlining both the positive and negative results. I also talked about some of the symptoms of the people who benefitted from the diet.

After the colloquium one of our graduate students, Susan, approached me to inquiry further about the dietary intervention. She stated that the symptoms I had talked about—mental confusion, depression, sweating unexpectedly, moodiness, etc.—were characteristic of her and that she would like to try the diet.

Susan completed the psychological test I developed as a selection tool and scored in the range which indicated she would benefit from the diet. I told her that her score indicated that she would profit from the diet and encouraged her to try it. She was asked to follow a specific set of procedures so that I could use her data as evidence of the effectiveness of the diet. She agreed to keep a record of her symptoms for two weeks (she actually kept them for 18 days) and then to follow the diet for two weeks again maintaining a record of her symptoms. After following the diet for two weeks Susan returned to her typical diet for two weeks and then again went back on the diet I had prepared.

One of the important aspects of this set of data was that Susan was a graduate student in our department and knew the importance of keeping good records and following instructions exactly. The results of Susan's data are in figure 4.3. From this figure you can see that she was experiencing many symptoms prior to dietary intervention (a phase that is called baseline), yet the number of symptoms she experienced gradually declined to zero when she was on the diet. When Susan returned to her old eating habits her symptoms began to return, then disappeared again when she followed the diet.

In looking at the return of Susan's symptoms when she returned to her old eating habits, it's obvious she didn't

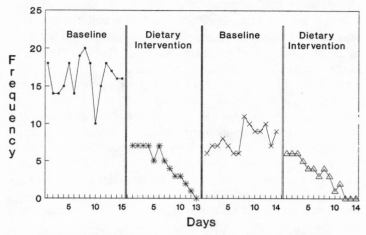

FIGURE 4.3 Frequency of symptoms experienced each day while eating a typical diet and during dietary intervention

feel as bad as she did during the initial baseline period. This is something I consistently find. It is easier, in most sensitive individuals, to get rid of symptoms than to cause them to return. Although I am not sure why this occurs, the symptoms return much slower than they are eliminated.

Refining the Dietary Intervention

Susan's data finally convinced me that the diet definitely was effective. Not only could symptoms be eliminated using the diet but the symptoms would return if old eating habits were reinstated. Although I was now convinced, there was still the nagging problem of expectancy. Susan knew when she was eating the diet I prescribed and when she went back to her old diet. Somehow I had to eliminate this knowledge.

I was also convinced I didn't need all the components of the high-protein, low-carbohydrate, caffeine and refined sucrose-free diet, so I started experimenting with it. I would have an individual follow this diet for two weeks and observe their symptoms disappear. Then I wanted to reintroduce into the diet some of the specific foods that had been eliminated to see if these foods caused a return of the symptoms and emotional distress. But which components of the diet should I reintroduce?

Most of the discussions I had read centered around refined sugar so I focused on this substance. I would have individuals follow the diet and observe their symptoms. When their symptoms disappeared I would have them drink Kool-Aid sweetened with refined sucrose (table sugar) or with the sweetener Equal. Some of these individuals experienced a return of their symptoms when drinking the sugar sweetened Kool-Aid but others did not. Now I was really confused and concerned. I was convinced sugar was the villain, at least for some individuals. But if it was, why did it not cause a return of the symptoms in all individuals? Was expectancy causing the benefit in those individuals who did not experience a return of symptoms when consuming the sugar?

Fortunately, an event happened that indicated sugar was not the only substance I should focus on. A co-ed in her 20s had just finished following the diet for two weeks. It had helped her tremendously. I asked her to drink some Kool-Aid sweetened with sugar and Kool-Aid sweetened with Equal but on different days. I didn't tell her which Kool-Aid drink she was getting on each of the different days so she could not develop an expectation. At the end of the second day, after drinking both Kool-Aid drinks, she still felt good and no symptoms had returned.

This was very frustrating. I could get rid of symptoms with the diet but I could not always get them to return by giving sugar. Why? I started talking to this individual about what she ate, how much she ate, and at what times. She stated she worked as a waitress at one of the local establishments. There was always a pot of coffee brewing and she drank several cups while at work. She also stated that the coffee seemed to have an effect on her. It seemed to make her feel jittery. Maybe this is the key! The diet eliminated beverages containing caffeine. Just maybe some of the individuals I had been experimenting with were caffeine sensitive rather than sucrose sensitive.

I asked her if she would mind drinking a cup of coffee to see if it had an effect on her. She agreed so I rushed down to the main office and poured a cup of coffee for her. She drank it and within half an hour she began to report the reappearance of several of her symptoms. Fantastic! Part of the mystery had been solved!

Although this fortunate discovery told me I must focus on caffeine as well as sugar, it obviously did not represent sound scientific evidence that eliminated the expectancy explanation. This expectancy explanation kept rearing its ugly head. Now I could focus on eliminating the expectancy hypothesis.

Ruling Out Expectancy

I focused on eliminating the expectancy explanation in two ways. In the first experiment, which again used a single subject design, I eliminated the expectancy explanation in the following manner: I first had Carol, a 21-year-old subject, complete several standardized psychological tests to obtain an indication of the degree of mood disturbance she was experiencing. These tests revealed she was experiencing a substantial degree of psychological distress consisting mostly of depression, anxiety, and nervousness. Then I asked her to follow a high-protein, low-carbohydrate diet void of sucrose, caffeine, and alcohol for two weeks. Then she completed the psychological tests again. This reassessment revealed that virtually all the psychological distress previously experienced was gone. No longer did Carol feel depressed, anxious, or nervous.

It was at this point that I implemented the controls for expectancy. I asked Carol to participate in a series of double-blind challenges consisting of several substances that had been eliminated in the diet she was given. I used caffeine and a variety of sweeteners in the challenges, but Carol was not informed of this. The double-blind challenges consisted of giving her a different sweetener, caffeine, or placebo on consecutive days.

Neither Carol nor the individual administering the caffeine or the sweeteners knew which was which because each substance was given in either a gelatin capsule or in water. In this way Carol could not develop a specific expectation related to taking a specific substance.

After taking each substance Carol provided a rating of any symptom she was experiencing at 5 minute intervals over a 40-minute time period. Although this challenge procedure did not indicate which substances were causing Carol's emotional distress, we did not tell her that. Rather, we told her the challenges revealed she was sensitive to saccharin and monosodium L-glutamate or MSG. She was told not to eat any foods with these substances in them for the next three weeks, but to add back to her diet other things such as caffeine products and sweets.

Carol was delighted. She really missed her sweets. Now she had the green light to start eating them again. She immediately went back to her apartment and baked some special goodies. Although Carol was delighted with the news that she could resume eating sweets and consuming caffeine, these substances were apparently causing her emotional distress. After three weeks of consuming these foods we gave her the psychological tests for a third time to assess her level of emotional distress. They revealed she was again beginning to show the same type of emotional distress she experienced prior to participating in the study. She was becoming depressed and her level of anxiety and nervousness was returning.

At last I had obtained evidence for the dietary intervention that was void of the expectation explanation. This was great. Even though I'd ruled out the expectation explanation, I was concerned that the challenges had not identified the offending substance. So I repeated the experiment on another person. The same procedure was used with Bob as with Carol. The results of this experiment paralleled Carol's. The dietary intervention produced a decrease in Bob's level of emotional distress; yet when he reintroduced caffeine and sugar back into his diet his emotional distress returned. More important, Bob also seemed to respond to the dietary challenges.

Thirty minutes following the sugar challenge Bob felt exhausted, weak, flighty, light-headed, and started developing a headache and upset stomach. He stated he started feeling *bad*. These feelings did not last very long, however. Bob was feeling better within an hour. The story is somewhat different with caffeine. About 30 minutes after consuming 100 milligrams of caffeine, an amount equal to about one cup of coffee or two cokes, Bob developed a moderately severe headache. He also experienced some degree of weakness, light-headedness, difficulty in concentration, nausea, tightness in his chest, flightiness, and a warm and dry mouth. When Bob returned the next day he requested we not give him the substance he received the prior day because he'd felt increasingly worse as the day progressed.

Extending the Challenges

Now I had even more evidence that the diet worked and that expectancy was not a factor. The challenges with caffeine and sugar had made Bob feel bad but none of the other challenge substances had. Even though Bob reacted to the challenges I had this nagging feeling that a 40-minute challenge, the length of time both Bob and Carol waited after consuming the caffeine and sugar, was not sufficient. Carol even stated that it took several days of eating sweets for her to start feeling worse.

I have now used the challenges with over 50 individuals and find that I need to increase the length of the challenges to at least 6 days to get an effect. In other words, a person has to consume one of the substances, such as sugar, for six consecutive days. Each day I measure their level of emotional distress. Even with the six-day challenge, some people don't experience a return of their previous level of emotional distress; others experience a return within a day or two.

Why some people react slower than others is still a mystery. I tend to believe certain individuals are just more sensitive to sugar and caffeine than others. Research also shows that protein can blunt the effect of sugar in some individuals. This may be why the challenges do not work with some subjects.

Refining the Dietary Intervention Again

Even though I had not totally solved the riddle of the challenges, I had revealed that the diet was effective and that sugar and caffeine seemed to be the primary foods that caused emotional distress. Now I had to verify I could get the same result by just taking sugar and caffeine out of the diet, as I was getting with a high-protein, low-carbohydrate, caffeine, and sugar-free diet.

I viewed this a being particularly important. The dietary challenges were indicating sugar and caffeine could reproduce symptoms. If these were the primary offending foods, then I should be able to make people feel better and eliminate their symptoms by just having them stop eating sugar, and drinking caffeine.

I have now conducted several experiments in which I have reduced the diet to eliminating sugar and caffeine. Interestingly, when I ask people to eliminate sugar and caffeine from their diet they experience the same benefit I observed from people who followed the high-protein, low-carbohydrate, caffeine and sugar-free diet.

Who Are These Dietary Responders?

By now I felt quite comfortable with the refinements I'd made in the diet. It was time to focus attention on other matters, such as identifying the characteristics of the dietary responders. Granted I had developed a psychological test that would select the sensitive person, but I wanted to know if these people had a specific set of personality characteristics or if they were distinguishable in any other manner. I also wanted to know if people with a specific psychiatric disorder would be responsive to dietary intervention.

One of my former graduate students, Kelly Krietsch (now a professor of psychology at Northern Arizona University), attempted to specify the type of person sensitive to the dietary intervention (I call these people dietary responders). To do this he first identified a group of people with a mood disturbance who profited from the dietary intervention (dietary responders) and a group of people with a mood disturbance who did not profit from the dietary intervention (dietary nonresponders). Then he gave both dietary responders and nonresponders several psychological tests and asked them to list the symptoms bothering them the most.

When we analyzed this data we found the dietary responders and nonresponders could not be distinguished on any of the psychological tests we had given them. Both groups were anxious, depressed, fatigued, mentally confused and generally emotionally disturbed. The dietary responders and nonresponders also did not differ in terms of the symptoms they said were bothering them. Both groups of people said they had problems with fatigue, headaches, nervousness, sleep, depression, moodiness, etc. It didn't make any difference how we analyzed the data. We couldn't find anything that distinguished the dietary responder from the nonresponder.

Although we couldn't identify characteristics that discriminated the dietary responder, the data consistently indicated that dietary responders as well as the nonresponders were depressed. Both groups not only had the symptoms of depression, but they also scored in the depressed range on our psychological tests. These finding were consistent with all the other studies we had conducted. I have found that dietary responders always experience some degree of depression.

This strongly suggested that a portion of clinically depressed individuals may also be dietary responders. I had always wanted to find out if people with a specific type of emotional disorder were dietary responders. The evidence

was building indicating that people with depression represented that type of person. My next step was to conduct
a study investigating the use of the dietary intervention
with people so severely depressed they would be classified
clinically depressed and need professional help.

CHAPTER 5

The Diet Eliminates Depression

Now that my research had demonstrated the benefits of the diet, I felt it was absolutely necessary to specify the type of emotionally disturbed person who may respond to the dietary intervention. This was essential so my professional colleagues could administer the dietary intervention to the right people. Granted, I had developed a psychological test that could pick out the dietary responder. However, it would be much more efficient to give this test only to certain types of individuals, such as those suffering from depression, and let it pick the dietary responder instead of having anyone experiencing emotional distress take the test. I also believed it was necessary to demonstrate that the emotional distress the dietary responders were experiencing was severe enough to require professional help.

With this in mind my next study was started. In this study individuals with major depression were used because my prior research indicated that dietary responders were depressed. I wanted to find out if individuals who were experiencing depression of sufficient severity to need professional help could be treated with the dietary intervention I had developed. Therefore, in this study only people who were so depressed they met the criteria for major depression, were used.

The Depression Study

Twenty such people volunteered to participate in this study. Now I had my clinical sample and could test the effectiveness of the diet on a group of individuals so emotionally distressed that they needed professional help. These 20 volunteers were randomly assigned to either an experimental group or a control group. The 10 people in the experimental group eliminated refined sugar and caffeine from their diet; the 10 people in the control group eliminated red meat and artificial sweeteners from their diet. The control group was asked to eliminate two substances from their diet so that they would be doing something similar to the experimental group in an attempt to make both groups equivalent in every respect except the foods they were eliminating.

The experimental and control volunteers were given a battery of psychological tests before starting their respective diets—and again three weeks after following their respective diets—to assess their depression and general level of psychopathology. The results were wonderful.

At the end of the three weeks only the experimental group that eliminated the sugar and caffeine demonstrated a significant decrease in their level of depression as well as their level of general psychopathology. The control group did not. These results of this study are summarized in Table 5.1 There you can see that 6 of the 10 people treated by eliminating sugar and caffeine were substantially improved after only three weeks of treatment and another 2 of the patients showed considerable improvement. This situation is reversed for those treated by eliminating red meat and artificial sweeteners.

One of the important facts that was not demonstrated in this study is that most of these individuals reported that most of their improvement occurred during the first week of treatment. This is virtually unheard of with other treatments of depression. Most treatments for depression take at least two to three weeks to even notice a substantial effect—and treatment lasts 8 to 12 weeks or longer.

Table 5.1
Status Of 20 Clinically Depressed Patients
After Three Weeks Of Dietary Treatment

Categories of patients after Dietary Intervention	Number treated by eliminating sugar and caffeine	Number treated by eliminating red meat and artificial sweeteners
Substantial Improvement with little if any depression remaining	6	1
Considerable improvement with some depression remaining	2	0
Little if any improvement	2	9

This study also demonstrated that eliminating sugar and caffeine does not eliminate depression in all individuals. It is not a panacea. Experience has shown that some individuals respond very rapidly to the elimination of refined sugar and caffeine. The depression begins to lift within the first three or four days. With other people it may take up to three weeks for the depression to lift. With yet other individuals, elimination of sugar and caffeine has no effect on the depression. Why some people's depression seems to be caused by eating sugar and/or caffeine is still a mystery. This does indicate that depression has many causes; diet is only one.

By now you may be thinking, "Can diet really do this? Can sugar and caffeine make me feel as depressed and miserable as I am? Can a dumb diet that eliminates sugar and caffeine really pull me out of this dark hole I seem to be in?" I have asked myself similar questions over the past eight years. The answer I have always come up with is, "Yes." Diet can have this effect and it can lift you out of the despair of depression.

The Case of Nancy

Nancy, one of the volunteers in the study I just mentioned, was a skeptic. She was feeling so bad when she came to see me and had tried so many other avenues, however, that she was desperate and willing to try anything. Fortunately, she followed the dietary intervention and her depression lifted within a few days. Because Nancy's case is so dramatic I think it is helpful to present a detailed account of it.

Her problems began shortly after the birth of her first child. Nancy began experiencing a series of flu-like symptoms. She would ache and feel run down and then the symptoms would disappear. But these flu-like symptoms reappeared almost every month.

About a year after the flu-like symptoms appeared Nancy started having weak, shaky spells which occurred without any warning and seemingly at random times. She could be talking on the phone, shopping, cooking, or doing anything when one of these spells would hit her. During this time she felt as though she had heart pains and her fingers, toes, and arms would tingle.

These symptoms caused her a great deal of concern so she made an appointment with her physician. To him, the symptoms suggested she may have hypoglycemia or maybe heart problems. So he scheduled her for a series of tests to check out these possibilities. The hypoglycemia test was, as the physician described it, *low normal,* or right on the borderline but not a problem. The other tests revealed Nancy had a slightly smaller than normal heart and a functional heart murmur. However, neither of these represented a problem and Nancy received a clean bill of health. In spite of this, she continued to experience the weak, shaky spells and the tingling sensations. But they were tolerable and she could live with them, which she did for the next seven years.

During the next year Nancy gave birth to her second child. Several months later things got worse. Nancy began experiencing nausea, chills, and sleepy spells every day after eating in the school cafeteria (she was an elementary school teacher) and occasionally at other times.

Since the symptoms did not disappear, Nancy made an appointment with her obstetrician and described her symptoms to him. He stated that it sounded like her hormones had not dropped back to a normal level since the birth of her second child and that she should give her body at least six months to straighten itself out. If it didn't straighten out by that time he would put her on birth control pills to regulate the hormones.

Six months later school was out and Nancy had the summer to relax. That summer Nancy moved to another state. The symptoms declined in intensity so she thought her body was beginning to straighten out and she'd soon be rid of the problem.

Unfortunately this was not the case. As soon as school started again the symptoms returned. Not only did they return but they became worse and new complaints appeared. Nancy not only experienced weakness and shakiness but now she had a continuous headache, blurred vision, a staggering gait, and sore muscles. She was unable to concentrate, and couldn't remember things. Her physician claimed her symptoms were due to moving from a relatively pollution-free environment to a heavily polluted one. He gave her medication for sinus headaches but they didn't help.

During the next six months her symptoms not only didn't improve, she added new ones—hot flashes and slurred speech. She made an appointment with another physician who hospitalized her for a variety of tests: brain tumor, epilepsy, diabetes and hypoglycemia. All the tests were negative except the CAT scan of her brain. This test revealed a tumor above the left eye which was the exact spot where her headaches were. More tests were scheduled for the next day to verify the results of the CAT scan.

That night Nancy could hardly sleep. She was petrified, yet relieved. The thought of a brain tumor terrified her, but at the same time she felt relief because she thought they had finally identified the problem. The subsequent tests revealed a benign cyst which was probably there before birth. She was given a diagnosis of migraine headaches—cause unknown.

Nancy's physician tried four different types of headache medication to try to give her relief from the excruciating headaches. None of them worked. She found that four extra-strength Tylenol did just as well and were much cheaper. Even with the Tylenol she continued to have the headaches but at least it provided some relief from the most severe ones. However, she had no respite from the other symptoms she endured. In spite of this, Nancy continued to teach and tried her best to be a good mother and wife.

Two months later Nancy went to school, walked into her classroom and found she could not remember any of her students' names! Their faces were familiar, but she couldn't recall a single name. Nancy just about panicked. She quickly picked up her roll sheet and started calling roll. When each student answered she would think "Oh, yes, that's who that child is." After school she rushed home and called her physician. When he answered she started crying and through her tears relayed the events of the day. Her physician referred her to a neurologist.

The day of her appointment she found she had trouble answering his questions because she couldn't think clearly. There seemed to be a long delay from the time a person asked her a question to the time she could answer it. She felt as though the spoken word had no meaning to her. When he asked her simple questions she even gave some wrong answers, such as the date of her birth. At times she would think one thing and state another—then feel bewildered by what she had just said. By this time Nancy thought she was going insane.

The tests revealed that, neurologically, Nancy was fine. But the neurologist believed her problem was her hormones because her symptoms were worse at mid-cycle and during her menstrual period. However, no hormone test was administered. Instead Nancy was given a diuretic to be taken at the middle of her menstrual cycle to flush the excess hormones out of her system. The diuretic seemed to help. Nancy began to function better, but she wasn't even close to being her normal self. At least she could now remember her student's names, although she still had trouble comprehending and not saying crazy, off-the-wall things.

Unfortunately, this improvement was short-lived. The next month more symptoms appeared. Now Nancy also felt tense, nervous, restless, fearful, apprehensive, agitated, and had a horrible temper with repeated flare-ups. She looked and felt very tired. She was no longer patient with her family or her students. Any little thing would provoke her.

Previously she had two qualities as a teacher that others always admired; patience and organizational skills. These qualities were gone. Not only were they gone, but Nancy's temper flared at teachers, students and her family. She was no longer an effective teacher because she couldn't organize her lesson plans, or paper work. She would start to teach something and forget the information she wanted to impart.

Two months later Nancy began feeling depressed. She attributed the depression to a recent miscarriage and to the guilt she felt because she was such a horrible wife, mother, daughter, teacher, friend, or anything else that she could think of. Nancy had finally reached the point where she no longer cared about anything, even how she looked.

In May of that year Nancy's husband's company sent them on a one-week vacation to England to entertain his clients. This should have been the highlight of the month for Nancy. But it wasn't. Instead of being happy and thrilled, she complained. To Nancy the vacation represented work and an expenditure of energy she didn't have. She saw the vacation as a chore. Even if someone else did the work of getting ready Nancy didn't feel like talking to anyone, especially engaging in happy chatter.

Somehow she managed to pack and went to England with her husband. However, after they arrived in England Nancy stayed in her room lying in bed with the drapes drawn tightly shut. She couldn't handle the noise and closeness of the sight-seeing tours. She was very happy to be alone in the comfort of the dark room. Her husband made excuses for her saying that she was not yet over her miscarriage.

About six months later Nancy became pregnant again. This was a very happy event. In fact, it was about the only happiness she saw in her life. She no longer wanted to go anywhere or do anything. She no longer found any enjoyment in reading, something she had always loved to do. By now Nancy had deteriorated to the point that she felt like life was a TV show and she was a passive viewer. There seemed to be an invisible barrier between herself and everyone else.

Nancy survived the school year only because she had two wonderful student teachers who took over many of the classroom responsibilities. However, this only placed another guilt on her ever expanding list. Now she was also a horrible supervising teacher.

Things had deteriorated so much that Nancy reached the conclusion that she could no longer handle being a wife, mother, and teacher—so she quit at the end of the year giving the excuse that she wanted to stay home with her baby. This was true, but it wasn't the whole truth. She felt like an alcoholic—trying to hide her condition from everyone. Nancy knew that if she taught another year, she would be exposed. It hurt deeply to give up teaching but she felt like she was doing the students a favor. They didn't need a teacher like her. That hurt too because she had wanted to be an elementary teacher ever since she was a child.

Nancy thought quitting teaching would solve all her problems. Now she would have to do only one job instead of two and she would have plenty of time to be a loving wife and mother. She thought that she would be the perfect housekeeper and cook. Well, maybe not perfect, but at least she would fix well-balanced meals and they would be on time and the laundry would be done. If only that had been the case. Instead of getting better Nancy got worse. In addition to the symptoms she was already experiencing she now lost her appetite and progressively lost weight. Her sexual desire declined and she felt extremely fatigued, exhausted, and very weak. Over the next three years these and the other symptoms gradually became severe. If it had not been for her husband and teenage daughter, there is no telling what would have become of her two young daughters. She couldn't get going or get organized.

Nancy could no longer function. She wasn't even capable of making out a grocery list. The only thing she did was watch the children. They were supervised. This heaped more guilt on Nancy. Here she was, home full time and she still could not function as a human being.

Thoughts of suicide entered her mind and gradually became a permanent part of her life even invading her dreams. She never at any time felt she would actually take her life. She thought of it only as a means of escaping and a way of freeing her family. The option of running away entered her mind, but she couldn't live without her family. She loved her family and wanted to be a good wife and mother, but she just didn't have the energy. If this was life, she didn't want to live, but she didn't want to die either. She just wanted to be human again.

At one point in time Nancy decided that maybe she was bored and needed something to do that would require a schedule so she decided to baby sit. She enjoyed the children she kept but physically it was just too taxing. After two months she felt like she had been baby sitting for two years without a break. Then her symptoms suddenly became even more severe.

Nancy overslept in the mornings because she woke up as tired as when she went to bed. She couldn't concentrate and was afraid she would let one of the children get hurt.

In December of that year she accidentally caused a fire because she forgot to turn off an appliance. She was afraid she would do that again. By now Nancy's hot flashes were so severe that when she was holding a child, the child would break out in a sweat.

Nancy's obstetrician prescribed Premarin because her hormone level tested low normal and he told her to keep a diary of all activities because he felt something in her environment was emotionally upsetting her, causing her symptoms. Nancy diligently kept the diary but it, like all the other tests she had taken, revealed nothing.

Nancy also quit driving unless it was absolutely necessary. Her judgment and slow, uncertain reflexes made it dangerous to drive a car. She even felt too weak to stand up long enough to take a shower.

In October Nancy made an appointment with an internist who tested her for Addison's disease, (she had all the symptoms, both general and specific) hypothyroidism, and electrolyte imbalance. Again the tests were all negative.

The internist ordered a CAT scan and X-rays for an upper GI series to check for cancer. Once again the tests showed nothing. At this point the internist felt that Nancy needed to see an endocrinologist because she was convinced that this was not just in Nancy's mind. She was the only physician that didn't write Nancy off, which made her feel good. However, Nancy didn't see an endocrinologist because they were still paying for their portion of the prior tests that had been conducted and Nancy felt that any test the endocrinologist would run would also be negative. She would gladly have paid any amount to get well, but they had already spent a small fortune and each time she was told she was healthy. This also made her feel guilty because the bills were taking money away from her family.

By March of the next year Nancy was crying all day long without any reason and her temper outbursts were unbearable. She lived in fear that she might physically hurt one of her children. She was afraid that sometime she might lose control and react without thinking. Nancy did scream at them a lot which added to her already excessive guilt.

Later that year Nancy read my advertisement for subjects for the depression study I was conducting. She almost didn't answer it because she thought, "Another dead end." But Nancy was desperate. She knew she had to get help quickly. It took her a week to even have enough energy to call and then two weeks to decide how she would be able to get to the psychology clinic. Who would take care of her daughter? When she finally did make an appointment and briefly relayed her symptoms and the fact that she felt as though her children did not have a mother, I told her "Maybe we can give your children their mother back." Nancy almost cried. She wanted that more than anything else because she felt that her two youngest daughters didn't know a different mother ever existed.

After her first appointment Nancy left the psychology clinic feeling very discouraged because she had no faith that a mere diet could change her life. Fortunately, she was desperate enough to try it. After only two days on the diet Nancy chuckled. Her whole family froze. She even shocked herself. It had been years since she had chuckled. By the end of the week Nancy was actually laughing. She awoke in the mornings feeling full of energy and so alive. She noticed for the first time in years that the sun was shining and even heard the birds singing. Life was taking on new meaning and she was glad to be part of it.

Nancy's case illustrates the tremendous benefit that can be achieved from following a few rather simple dietary guidelines. This does not mean everyone who suffers from depression can expect to receive the same degree of benefit. Not everyone can. As I mentioned earlier, depression has many causes and improper diet is only one of them. Some people may experience depression for a number of different reasons; diet may be only one of the contributing causes.

I have treated numerous individuals who profited from the diet. For some, even after the diet had its effect, there was still some residual depression. Such individuals need traditional psychotherapy in addition. Diet is not a panacea. Don't take this to mean that diet doesn't help a lot of people because it can and it does. For those who are sensitive to sugar and/or caffeine, eliminating these substances from their fare can change their lives. They will feel better, be more optimistic, and enjoy a fuller and richer life.

PART II

INVESTIGATING THE FOOD-MOOD CONNECTION

CHAPTER 6

Should You Try the Diet?

By now you know that the essential ingredients of the dietary intervention are the elimination of sugar and caffeine. This sounds simple and it really is. But it is not quite as simple as it appears. There are many subtle issues to be considered and steps to be followed to insure that you get maximum benefit.

I remember a woman who called me to inquire about the studies I had been conducting. She said she had read about my work in a recent newspaper article. From our conversation I learned that this woman experienced some depression, and she was very moody, especially just before the beginning of her menstrual cycle. From talking to her it seemed as though her symptoms were due to diet. Then I learned her physician had said her problem could be diet and that she should eliminate sugar. The woman said that she was following the physician's advice and that she did feel somewhat better although depression, moodiness, and fatigue were still a problem.

When someone tells me this I always get that twinge of uncertainty. Did she really eliminate sugar. And if she did why is she still having the symptoms? Then she made a very revealing statement. She said she had just reduced her sugar consumption but had not totally eliminated it from her diet. Now things were beginning to make sense.

Many times people think if they just reduce their sugar or caffeine consumption the effects of this substance will be eliminated. That is true for some people but not for others. It is these small components of the dietary intervention that are important to its success.

Will You Respond to the Diet?

Lets assume you're feeling down in the dumps, have a very low self image, are moody and tired, and just feel terrible most of the time. In other words, you are depressed. Is the diet for you? Will the diet pull you out of your deep dark hole and make you feel human again? Will the diet bring you back to the point that you will enjoy life again and have a desire to live?

There are several questions you can ask yourself that will help you make this decision. Go over each of the following questions and, if the answer to most of them is yes, then it's very possible diet is partially or totally responsible for the way you feel.

1. When you feel *low*, down in the *dumps*, or depressed, is there a specific reason for it or can you be in a situation in which you are having a good time and then, all of a sudden, feel a wave of depression engulf you?

Many times dietary responders report they have these feelings of depression for unknown reasons. They feel miserable for no apparent reason. It is as though they climb into this deep dark hole at times and they can't control when or why it happens. If this situation describes you it is one indication that you may be a dietary responder or that the depression you are experiencing is caused by diet. On the other hand, if this situation doesn't describe you, it does not necessarily mean you are not a dietary responder.

Some dietary responders can identify specific situations that seem to be causing their depression. Linda was one of those individuals. When I first saw Linda, she stated that her son, daughter-in-law, and ex-husband were all living with her. All these people were mooching off of her. She was providing food and shelter for them—yet they did little or nothing to help her clean the house, cook, or even do the dishes after she prepared the meal. To make matters worse, she paid most of the bills. Yet they would criticize her for being selfish and not thinking of them. They constantly asked more and more of her and she would never tell them no! Linda was unable to confront them and demand that they help or leave. She felt worthless; nothing she did was good enough. To Linda, this was the cause of her depression.

Without inquiring further it would have been easy to attribute her depression to this unhealthy family situation. Further questioning, however, revealed that Linda—who currently was in her 60s, had experienced depression since she was a young woman. Linda had, throughout her adult life, periodically received counseling for her depression. At the time I saw her she was in counseling with another psychologist and taking antidepressant medication prescribed by a psychiatrist. The important issue for me was that Linda's depression was not just tied to her current family situation but that she had experienced depression prior to this time. This suggested that the diet might be beneficial to her.

I encouraged her to follow it closely which she agreed to do. Within two weeks Linda's depression began to lift. As her despondent mood lifted she decreased her antidepressant medication. She didn't like taking it anyway because it made her mouth and hair dry. She eventually quit taking the antidepressant medication and her depression continued to improve as long as she stayed on the diet. Linda also found other side benefits to the dietary intervention. As her mood improved she became more assertive with her free-loading family and insisted they contribute their fair share.

Linda's case clearly illustrates a situation in which the dietary intervention helped eliminate her depression. This also illustrates a situation where traditional psychotherapy was also needed. No amount of dietary intervention could eliminate the unhealthy family interactions. She needed continued counseling to help her deal with her kids and ex-husband.

Unfortunately, Linda not only did not receive the counseling she needed, but she gradually started drinking coffee again. As her coffee consumption increased her depression returned. About a year after I had first treated her, I began another study and was advertising for volunteers. Linda contacted me about being a volunteer because her depression had returned. I had to tell her that she had participated once and that meant that we could not use her again. I then asked her about her diet. This is when she told me she had started drinking coffee again and that her depression returned as her coffee consumption increased.

Linda's case illustrates that you should not dismiss diet even if there seems to be a specific cause of depression. When a specific cause can be identified you must ask yourself if the depression existed prior to this presumed cause or if the depression only occurs following some legitimate cause. If your low mood existed prior to some stressful situation, diet may be the cause of much of the depression being experienced.

Many times a person may be mildly depressed as a result of their diet and this level of depression may exist prior to some stressful situation such as a divorce. When the stressful situation is imposed on top of the mild depression, the depression worsens. In such a situation diet can still help reduce the depression and it is important this solution is not dismissed. *Try the diet*. It can't hurt and it frequently helps. The help it provides is often substantial.

2. Do you feel as though you are very moody?

Dietary responders frequently view themselves as being moody people. They get irritated and angry very easily. They cry easily. Or they feel fairly good one moment—and the next they can feel awful.

A woman called me one day inquiring about my work and said that she had two beautiful daughters who seemed to fit the profile of a dietary responder. I encouraged her to have them make an appointment to see me. One of her daughters, Ann called the next week.

Ann's mother was certainly correct. Ann was an attractive brunette in her mid 20s, married with one child. During the initial interview Ann revealed she felt depressed much of the time. She also reported she was quite intolerant of little things her husband did and that they frequently argued. Ann felt as though she was very moody and had a short fuse. She would fly off the handle and get mad at insignificant things. Her anger was so intense at times she felt as though she would get *killing mad.*

After Ann had been on the diet for two weeks her depression lifted and her moodiness and anger virtually disappeared. This is not to say she never got mad because she did. Only now she was not as quick to anger. She was more tolerant and had a better marriage.

Then I challenged Ann with caffeine. I gave her caffeine-filled gelatin capsules to see if she was sensitive to this substance. When I talked to her at the end of the sixth challenge day she told me if she didn't get off this substance her husband was going to divorce her. Ann's moodiness, short fuse, and anger had returned. This was a case of caffeine rather than sugar causing the depression, moodiness, and anger.

3. Are you tired and fatigued most of the time? Can you sleep eight or more hours a night yet wake up tired? Do you ever feel as though the energy is suddenly being drained out of you?

This experience of fatigue and being sapped of energy is very characteristic of dietary responders. Individuals with this persistent fatigue seem to have little motivation. They'll do virtually anything to get out of doing work. They appear lazy, which is very irritating to those around them. Others frequently feel as though all this person needs is a swift kick in the rear to motivate them. However, the real reason behind the apparent laziness and lack of motivation is extreme and persistent fatigue. These people don't have the energy to do anything.

4. Do you have frequent headaches?

Although headaches are not one of the most dominant symptoms of dietary responders, they occur with sufficient frequency to be included as an indicator. Dietary responders often report experiencing headaches several times a week; some have them almost every day. The headaches range from a dull ache to something approaching a migraine. There is no consistent pattern.

Frequent headaches are one indicator that your depression may be due to diet. However, you should not use headaches as the primary indicator. You must have other symptoms such as the fatigue, moodiness, and depression along with the headache to qualify as a good candidate for being a dietary responder. These symptoms must be there most of the time, not just when you have a headache.

Individuals who suffer from periodic migraines may also experience moodiness, fatigue and depression when the migraine occurs. The important point to ask yourself is whether these symptoms exist even when you *don't* have the migraine.

Let's assume that you've read each of the above questions and you agree with most of them. You feel depressed, you're tired most of the time, quite moody, and frequently have a dull headache. This means you may be a dietary responder. I say *may* be because a positive answer to these questions is only an indication. Try the diet. You have nothing to lose by trying it and everything to gain. The diet is definitely not going to harm you and may do you a world of good.

CHAPTER 7

So What Is the Diet?

The diet I have used in my most recent studies and the one that has worked well appears in table 7.1. You can see the diet consists essentially of selecting foods that are void of refined sucrose and caffeine.

Table 7.1 merely presents a partial list of foods void of sugar and caffeine. You could select others. If you deviate from the foods listed in this table you *must* read the label to insure that no caffeine or sugar is included.

Some labels, rather than stating that the item contains sugar or refined sucrose will say it contains dextrose or glucose. If these sweeteners are included I would also recommend you avoid that food. While I have not directly investigated these sweeteners, they are also sugars and may be equally harmful. The best bet is to play it safe until you find out if diet is all or part of your problem and which dietary substance is causing the problem.

If the food contains fructose or corn sweeteners you may be able to handle this sweetener. Fructose is metabolized slower than sugar and apparently is tolerated fairly well by most individuals sensitive to sugar. While it may be tolerated better, I still suggest you avoid this sweetener as much as possible until you have identified the benefit you receive from eliminating caffeine and sugar.

Table 7.1
List of Acceptable Foods
Without Caffeine and Refined Sucrose

BREAKFAST

Cereals — Oatmeal, Shredded Wheat, Grape Nuts, Kellogg's Nutri-Grain Cereals (Wheat, Corn, Barley and Rye), Wheatena.

Eggs

Toast

Milk

Juice — Any variety made from frozen concentrate (Not a juice drink like Tang).

Butter — or Margarine

Honey — On toast or cereal but in moderate amounts

Sweetener — Equal or Nutrasweet

LUNCH AND DINNER

Meat — Chicken, fish, turkey or any red meat (do not eat Bar-B-Que).

Vegetable — Any variety as long as it is fresh or frozen (do not eat canned vegetables).

Salad — Prepare using any type of lettuce or other fresh fruits and vegetables.

Fruit — Any fresh fruit (do not eat canned fruits).

Salad dressings — Use Marie's brand salad dressing (Blue Cheese, Avocado Goddess, or Italian Garlic) or use vinegar and oil.

Potatoes — Rice, etc. are acceptable.

Beverages — Milk, water, or any juice such as apple, orange, grapefruit, etc. made from a concentrate and not sweetened.

Sandwiches — Tuna, cheese, hamburger.

Sweetener — The only acceptable ones are Equal or Nutrasweet and Saccharin.

Avoid prepackaged or prepared meals!

EATING OUT

It is recommended you don't eat out for two weeks or until you have received the benefit from the dietary intervention and have identified the dietary substance or substances that are causing the mood disturbance.

If you must eat out be sure to determine if sugar has been included in any of the items you might select such as salad dressing. Restaurants add sugar to many items and it is necessary to inquire about each one.

In general, Mexican food is the most acceptable food because this food is prepared in such a manner that corresponds closely to the demands of the dietary program.

SNACKS

Pretzel sticks, cheese, Saltine crackers, Triscuit wafers, popcorn (plain with salt or butter if desired), any type of fruit such as apples, nuts or seeds of any kind such as peanuts, plain or nonfat yogurt.

HEADACHE MEDICATION

Any type such as Tylenol as long as it does not contain caffeine.

Although Table 7.1 provides a partial list of foods to select from for each of your three daily meals, some people feel lost when they are first confronted with the idea of eating only foods without sugar. The addition of sugar in foods so permeates our society that the transition to sugar-free eating is difficult for some. For this reason most people find a sample meal plan to be helpful.

Table 7.2
Sample Meal Plan Void
of Refined Sucrose and Caffeine

BREAKFAST

Two eggs scrambled in margarine
Wheat toast with margarine
Grits or hash brown potatoes
Beverage

LUNCH

Tuna—water packed
Celery
Bread
Fruit
Beverage
Yogurt—plain unsweetened (add vanilla for flavor)

EVENING MEAL

Fresh spinach salad
Marie's salad dressing or vinegar and oil
Broiled pork loin
Cooked peas
Asparagus spears
Margarine—served on vegetables
Bread with margarine or butter
Beverage

In following this diet the important issue is to make sure you don't eat sugar or caffeine. You can have unlimited variety in your meals. Just *make sure they do not contain sugar, dextrose, glucose, or caffeine.*

While I have focused most attention on the fact that sugar is included in so many foods, I haven't said much about caffeine. Most of us realize caffeine is included in beverages like coffee and tea. However, caffeine is an ingredient in many other drinks such as the soda, Mountain Dew. It is also included in many over-the-counter medications and prescription drugs, as well as anything with chocolate in it. The following tables provide lists of the substances that contain caffeine.

Table 7.3
Caffeine Content of Beverages

Type	Amount	Average Caffeine
Coffee		
Drip, automatic	5 ounces	137 mg.
Drip, manual	5 ounces	124 mg.
Instant	5 ounces	60 mg.
Instant, decaffeinated	5 ounces	3 mg.
Percolated, automatic	5 ounces	117 mg.
Percolated, manual	5 ounces	108 mg.
Coffee, Flavored Instant Mixes		
Cafe amaretto	6 ounces	60 mg.
Cafe francais	6 ounces	52 mg.
Cafe vienna	6 ounces	57 mg.
Irish mocha mint	6 ounces	27 mg.
Orange cappucino	6 ounces	74 mg.
Sunrise (coffee & grain)	6 ounces	37 mg.
Suisse mocha	6 ounces	40 mg.
Coffee, Instant Dry Powder		
regular	1 teaspoon	60 mg.
freeze dried	1 teaspoon	60 mg.
coffee with grain	1 teaspoon	56 mg.
decaffeinated	1 teaspoon	3 mg.
Tea		
Am. black, 1 min brew	5 fl. ounces	28 mg.
Am. black, 3 min	5 fl. ounces	42 mg.
Am. black, 5 min	5 fl. ounces	46 mg.
black, imported, 5 min	5 fl. ounces	65 mg.

decaffeinated, 5 min	5 fl. ounces	1 mg.
green, 1 min brew	5 fl. ounces	4 mg.
green, 3 min brew	5 fl. ounces	27 mg.
green, 5 min brew	5 fl. ounces	31 mg.
instant	5 fl. ounces	33 mg.
mint flavor, 5 min brew	5 fl. ounces	50 mg.
orange & spice, 5 min	5 fl. ounces	45 mg.
oolong, 1 min brew	5 fl. ounces	13 mg.
oolong, 3 min brew	5 fl. ounces	30 mg.
oolong, 5 min brew	5 fl. ounces	40 mg.

Tea, Instant Dry Powder

regular	1 teaspoon	32 mg.
lemon flavored	1 teaspoon	38 mg.

Table 7.4
Caffeine Content of Medications

Type	mg/tablet, capsule, or dose (dose=/d)

Non-Prescription Drugs

Alpha-phed/beta phed	32
Anacin Analygesic/Anacin max strength/Anacin-3	32
Aqua-Ban (diuretic)	200/d
B-A-C/B-A-C #3 (headache)	40
Bromoquinine (for colds)	15
Caffedrine Capsules (stimulant)	200/d
Cenegisic (for cold/allergy)	15
Cope (for pain)	32
Coryban-D (for colds)	30
Dristan/Dristan A-F (decongestant)	16
Efed (stimulant)	200
Excedrin (for pain)	65
G-1	40
Gelpurin	32
Goody's Headache Powder (for pain)	33/d
Medigesic Plus	40
Midol (for pain/diuretic)	32
Neo-synephrine (for cold/allergy)	15
No Doz (stimulant)	100
Orphengesic	30
Orphengesic Forte	60
Permathene Water Off (diuretic)	200/d
Pre-Mens Forts (diuretic)	100/d
Prolamine (weight control)	140
Sinapils (for Allergy)	32
Sinarest (for Allergy)	30
Synalgos-DC (for pain)	30
Tencet	40
Triaminicin (for colds)	30
Tussirex	25
Vanquish (for pain)	33
Vivarin tablets (stimulant)	200

Prescription Drugs

Cafergot capsules (migraine headaches)	100
Damason (pain)	32
Darvon Compound (pain reliever)	32
Esgic tablets (sedative/analgesic)	40
Fioricet (headache)	40
Fiorinal tablets (headaches)	40
Migrol tablets (headaches)	50
Migralam capsules (migraine headaches)	100
Norgesic (pain)	30
Soma Compound (pain reliever/muscle relaxant)	32
Wigraine (headache)	100

Table 7.5
Caffeine Content of Chocolate
and Foods Containing Chocolate

Type	Amount	Average Caffeine
Baking chocolate	1 ounce	35 mg
Baking chocolate, Baker's	1 ounce	25 mg
Baking chocolate, Hershey	1 ounce	26 mg
Chocolate Candy		
Baker's chocolate flavored chips,	¼ cup	12 mg
Baker's chocolate, German, sweet,	1 ounce	8 mg
Chocolate kisses	6 pieces	5 mg
Crunch bar, Nestle's	1.06 oz. bar	7 mg
Golden almond	1 ounce	5 mg
Kit kat	1½ oz. bar	5 mg
Krackel bar	1.2 oz. bar	5 mg
Milk chocolate	1 ounce	6 mg
Hershey's milk chocolate	1.05 oz. bar	5 mg
Nestle's milk chocolate	1.07 oz. bar	8 mg
Hershey's milk chocolate, w/almonds	1.05 oz. bar	5 mg
Nestle's milk chocolate, w/almonds,	1 ounce	6 mg
Milk chocolate chips	¼ cup	8 mg
Mr. Goodbar	1.65 oz. bar	6 mg
Reese's peanut butter cup	2 pieces	4 mg
Baker's sweet German chocolate	1 ounce	8 mg
Rolo	5 pieces	1 mg
Hershey's semi-sweet chocolate	¼ cup	4 mg
Nestle's semi-sweet chocolate	1 ounce	17 mg
Sweet (dark) chocolate	1 ounce	20 mg
Hershey's special dark chocolate	1.02 oz. bar	23 mg
Thousand dollar bar	1½ oz. bar	5 mg
Whatchamacallit	1.1 oz. bar	1 mg
Chocolate brownie with nuts	1¼ oz.	8 mg
Chocolate cake	1/10 of 9"	14 mg
Chocolate covered candy	1 ounce	3 mg
Chocolate ice cream	⅔ cup	5 mg
Chocolate fudge topping	2 T	5 mg
Chocolate milk	8 fl. oz.	5 mg
Chocolate powder for milk	1 T	10 mg

Hershey's chocolate powder for milk	3 T	6 mg
Nestle's Quik chocolate milk powder	2 T	7 mg
Chocolate pudding from instant mix	½ cup	6 mg
D-Zerta low-cal chocolate pudding	½ cup	5 mg
Chocolate pudding pop	1 pop	4 mg
Chocolate tapioca pudding, from mix	½ cup	9 mg
Chocolate syrup	2 T	4 mg
Cocoa beverage	6 fl. oz.	5 mg
Cocoa, dry, powder	1 T	11 mg
Cocoa, dry, Hershey's	1 ounce	70 mg
Cocoa mix, Hershey's	1 pkt.	5 mg
Cocoa mix, Nestle's	1 ounce	4 mg
Cocoa mix, w/marshmallows, Nestle's	1 ounce	4 mg

Table 7.6
Caffeine Content of Soft Drinks

Type	Amount	Average Caffeine
Aspen	12 fl. oz.	36 mg
Big Red	12 fl. oz.	38 mg
Big Red, Diet	12 fl. oz.	38 mg
Canada Dry Jamaica cola	12 fl. oz.	30 mg
Coca-Cola	12 fl. oz.	45 mg
Cola/pepper sodas	12 fl. oz.	40 mg
Cola soda, decaffeinated	12 fl. oz.	trace
Cola soda, decaffeinated, diet	12 fl. oz.	trace
Diet Coke	12 fl. oz.	45 mg
Diet-Rite Cola	12 fl. oz.	36 mg
Dr. Pepper	12 fl. oz.	40 mg
Dr. Pepper, Diet	12 fl. oz.	40 mg
Kick	12 fl. oz.	31 mg
Mountain Dew	12 fl. oz.	54 mg
Mr. Pibb	12 fl. oz.	41 mg
Mr. Pibb, Diet	12 fl. oz.	57 mg
Mello Yello	12 fl. oz.	53 mg
Pepsi Cola	12 fl. oz.	38 mg
Pepsi, Diet	12 fl. oz.	36 mg
Pepsi Light	12 fl. oz.	36 mg
Royal Crown Cola	12 fl. oz.	36 mg
Royal Crown Cola, Diet	12 fl. oz.	33 mg
Royal Crown with a twist	12 fl. oz.	21 mg
Shasta Cola	12 fl. oz.	44 mg
Shasta Cherry Cola	12 fl. oz.	44 mg
Shasta Diet Cola	12 fl. oz.	44 mg
Shasta Diet Cherry Cola	12 fl. oz.	44 mg
Tab	12 fl. oz.	45 mg
Jolt	12 fl. oz.	73 mg

From the preceding tables you can see that many foods and medications contain caffeine and many of them give no indication that caffeine is one of their ingredients. For this reason you must be cautious and read the labels of everything you consume to insure that it is free of caffeine and sugar. (Note: there are some soft drinks now available that are both caffeine and sugar free.)

CHAPTER 8

Issues to Consider
in Following the Diet

For many people, eliminating refined sucrose and caffeine from their diet is not as simple as it appears. Many foods and medications include these substances and it is necessary to read the label of virtually everything you put in your mouth to make sure neither of these substances are included. For example, many medications not only contain caffeine but may also contain sugar to reduce their bitter taste. If the medication is a prescription drug you may not get the information describing the ingredients. Ask your pharmacist if the medication contains sugar or caffeine.

If you're committed to trying the sugar and caffeine-free diet I presented in the last chapter, there are several issues you must be aware of because they can affect the success of the diet and your ability to stick to it.

Staying on the Diet

One of the first issues is that you *must* stick to the diet. Absolutely no deviations, at least initially. This means totally eliminating sugar and caffeine. There are some people who can benefit from just reducing their caffeine and sugar intake, but there's no way of determining if you are one of these people.

You could try cutting down and see if your symptoms disappeared. If they did then you would know you could tolerate some sugar or caffeine, but more than a certain amount would bring on the symptoms. However, assume you just reduced your intake and your symptoms did not go away. Is it because you're not sugar and/or caffeine sensitive—or because you are *extremely* sensitive and must totally eliminate these substances in order to feel good? You can't answer this question without totally eliminating both.

There are people who can reduce their sugar and/or caffeine intake and feel better. The severity of their symptoms will have declined. When they consume sugar or caffeine their symptoms return. Because the severity of their symptoms declined when they reduced their intake, these people are often deluded into thinking that a small amount of sugar or caffeine is okay, but larger amounts are not.

Joan was one such individual. When I first saw Joan she was depressed and very anxious. She couldn't sit still. She was always squirming in her chair, crossing her legs, bouncing her foot, or playing with her hair. She knew she was sensitive to sugar because she would develop symptoms such as mental confusion if she ate a donut or a piece of pie. She never associated her depression or nervousness with sugar. Joan had to totally eliminate sugar to see that this food was not only responsible for these symptoms, but it was also causing her depression and nervousness. After being on a sugar-free diet for two weeks her depression and nervousness were almost totally gone. When we challenged her with sugar they immediately returned.

When you eliminate sugar and caffeine from your diet it is important that you substitute other foods for them. Don't stop eating or dramatically reduce your food consumption just because now you don't eat sugar or drink caffeine. Doing so can be harmful mentally and physically.

Semi-starvation
Is Psychologically and Physically Unhealthy

About six months ago I received a letter from a woman who had read a press release about my work. In her letter she stated she had been dieting all of her life and that she was desperate to lose weight. Her goal was 118 pounds. She currently fluctuated from 123 to 133 pounds.

The last four months she had become very depressed and often considered driving off an embankment to end her life. She was obsessed with trying to lose weight, even to the detriment of her physical and mental health. Her solution was to starve herself. She was to the point where she was not eating at all Monday through Friday. The only nourishment she would have was from the diet sodas she drank. If you look at the contents of a diet soda there is very little nourishment in them.

Her rationale was that she had been placed behind a desk answering a phone. "So I figured, no movement, no calories burnt, no need to eat." Then on the weekend she would binge, eating tremendous amounts of food. After that she'd feel guilty and throw up to purge the food. This woman had obviously developed a very unhealthy pattern of eating. While her lack of eating was not due to elimination of sugar and/or caffeine, it does illustrate the inappropriate behavior patterns people sometimes develop. It is okay to reduce food intake but you must not starve yourself! Eat a balanced diet.

Several studies have documented the psychological effects of semi-starvation. The most descriptive and classic one was conducted at the University of Minnesota many years ago. It identified the effectiveness of several different diets in bringing about recovery from semi-starvation.

To investigate recovery it was necessary to have a group of volunteers go on a semi-starvation diet. Thirty males between the ages of 20 and 33 volunteered to participate in a six-month study which reduced their daily dietary intake to 1,570 calories. This caloric intake was not sufficient to maintain their normal weight; the volunteers gradually lost 24 percent of their normal weight.

Over a six-month period these volunteers experienced many physical and psychological changes. They naturally became thin and their faces and bodies appeared emaciated. From a psychological perspective, the interesting point is that these volunteers changed in a way that appears very much like that of a depressed person. The volunteers experienced periods of despondency ranging from a temporary depressive episode to prolonged periods of depression. In addition to feeling remorse, they became more irritable and had short tempers.

Their personal appearance deteriorated. They often neglected to shave, brush their teeth, or even comb their hair. The men became indecisive. They were unable to plan events, to participate in group activities, and generally could not make decisions. Their interest in other people and events dropped off dramatically. It was just *too much trouble* or *too tiring* to have to contend with other people. Sexual feelings and expression became almost nonexistent. The number of dates plummeted; those who continued to date found that their relationships were strained. One of the volunteers stated "I have no more sexual feeling than a sick oyster."

Studies such as this illustrate the extensive psychological impact semi-starvation can have on a person. While I'm not suggesting you may starve yourself to the extent that the volunteers did, such studies illustrate what starvation can do. Even temporary starvation, like going on a four-day crash diet, can have similar though less extreme effects. Eat a good balanced diet and don't reduce your calorie intake beyond that necessary to function adequately.

Some of you may be concerned about weight loss. This is natural. My recommendation is to delay that concern until you have eliminated your depression. Then you will be better equipped to work on the weight loss. It may be that elimination of sugar from your diet will result in some weight loss. This happens fairly frequently, although it does not occur with everyone.

Caffeine Withdrawal Headache

When following the sugar and caffeine-free diet, be prepared to experience withdrawal. The most common withdrawal effect is a headache. Many people who follow the diet get a headache, which is probably caused by the elimination of caffeine.

Caffeine causes the blood vessels in the brain to constrict. Withdrawal of caffeine eliminates this constriction and allows the blood vessels to dilate and return to their normal state. If you've been a repeated and constant caffeine consumer, the constricted state would represent the normal state of the blood vessels in your brain. When you eliminate caffeine the blood vessels appear to dilate, but this is just a return to their normal caffeine-free state. This suggests the resulting headache is due to the elimination of the caffeine.

Such headaches can be very severe in some people. One woman I treated had a caffeine withdrawal headache so painful it put her to bed for several days. Others have headaches so acute they say they are intolerable and want to quit the diet. These individuals have to gradually eliminate caffeine rather than go it *cold turkey.* Fortunately, only a few people have such a severe reaction.

Although the caffeine withdrawal headache can be quite severe, it doesn't last long in most individuals. In most cases it will disappear within three to four days. When it does last longer, the first several days are typically the worst. Gradually the headache diminishes over the next week or two. Aspirin without caffeine or Tylenol can be taken for the headache, but most people report it does little good. The best remedy is time.

Some individuals experience no caffeine withdrawal headache. The amount of caffeine a person is consuming is no indicator. Nancy was drinking about 20 cups of coffee a day prior to beginning the dietary intervention. I warned her of the possibility of having a caffeine withdrawal headache and that it should last only three or four days if it occurred.

Although I didn't tell Nancy, I was very concerned because of the tremendous amount of caffeine she was consuming. If the withdrawal headache was based on the amount of caffeine consumed she should have a whopper, because she was consuming an excessive amount!

When I saw her the next week I asked her if she had experienced a headache. Much to my surprise she said no. Betty had just the opposite experience. Prior to Betty's starting the diet she was drinking only three or four cups of coffee a day. Yet her withdrawal headache was so bad we had to gradually eliminate her caffeine consumption.

Subjective Symptoms

During the first several days or weeks on the diet, some people report experiencing some light-headedness or shakiness between meals. If such symptoms occur it's important to eat something immediately. Try an apple, a piece of cheese, or some nuts. This should reduce the severity of the symptoms. If these symptoms continue to occur for several days you should record when they occur and then eat something about half-an-hour prior to their occurrence. This should eliminate them in the future. As time goes by, these symptoms should disappear and you can eliminate the snack without a problem.

How Fast Does the Diet Work

When people start the diet, one of the first things they want to know is how long it's going to take for them to get relief. While you can't expect to get relief within a few hours, most people can within a few days.

Kriki was one of my more severe clients. She ran the whole gamut of symptoms: depression, crying, fatigue, mental confusion, indecisiveness, feelings of worthlessness, etc. When she started the diet I told her it may take several weeks to get rid of her depression and the other symptoms she was experiencing. Either she did not hear me or was so desperate to get aid that when she did not feel better within 24 hours she started becoming discouraged and doubted the usefulness of the diet. She came back to my office and complained that all the symptoms were still there. She didn't feel any better. I encouraged her to give the diet time to work.

The next day the same thing happened. She was again in my office. I again told her to be patient and stick rigidly to the diet. The third day the same thing happened again. Then I didn't see her on the fourth day or the fifth day. When Kriki returned at her regularly scheduled appointment one week after beginning the diet she exclaimed, "Dr. Christensen, on the fourth day I suddenly started feeling better." She could almost identify the hour when things turned around for her. Others have mentioned similar experiences. One person said when she woke up one morning she felt like a new person. The fatigue and depression were gone.

While some people seem to be able to identify the specific time that their symptoms started disappearing, others cannot. For them it is a gradual process with the symptoms slowly diminishing. This time period can last anywhere from three days to about two weeks. Because of the variability in response to the diet, a rule of thumb I use is that you must stay on the diet for at least two to three weeks to see if it is going to be of benefit for you.

Caffeine or Sugar—Which Is the Problem?

Whenever I talk about my research and mention the diet, I naturally state that it involves elimination of sugar and caffeine. This suggests that the people who benefit from the diet are sensitive to both of these substances. For some people this is true. Some people are sensitive to both substances. However, this is the exception rather than the rule. In most cases a person is bothered by either sugar or caffeine—only one of these substances is causing their symptoms.

At this point you might be asking, "Why have I insisted that both caffeine and sugar be eliminated? Why not just eliminate the one a person is sensitive to?" This is a very legitimate question. If it were possible to identify beforehand which substance a person was sensitive to then only one needs to be eliminated. The problem is that I don't know of any way to identify the offending element.

The reason I insist on eliminating both substances is that, if you first eliminated one and it was not the offender, you might get discouraged with the diet and not try eliminating the other substance. Then you would not have identified which was causing your problem. Also, if you eliminate the wrong one first it delays your getting relief.

This does not mean you can't eliminate one substance and then the other. You can. Just make sure you eliminate both sugar and caffeine before you conclude diet is not the cause of your symptoms. If you decide to take this strategy, first eliminate sugar. More of the people I have treated are sugar sensitive.

Identifying the Culprit
Using the Challenge Procedure

If you decide to follow the dietary program I suggest, eliminate both caffeine and sugar. After your depression has lifted, you need to identify the substance that caused it. You can do this through a process of challenging your body with each of the substances. This means you ingest one substance and see what reaction you get. If you start eating sugar and your depression, fatigue, mental confusion, and moodiness return—then sugar is a problem and you must stay away from it. Similarly, if you start consuming caffeine again and this makes you feel depressed, anxious, nervous, and sleepless, this is an indication you are sensitive to caffeine.

Lets assume you've tried the diet and, much to your pleasant surprise, it works. After two weeks your energy has returned, your mood has lifted and you feel good again. Now you want to find out if the culprit is sugar or caffeine. I recommend testing for caffeine first because the sugar challenge can be a little more complex.

Probably the best way to challenge your body with caffeine is to buy No-Doz tablets or some other similar over-the-counter stimulant because these tablets contain primarily caffeine. If you take these tablets you can find out how your body reacts to caffeine uncontaminated by anything else. Take an amount of caffeine approximately equal to what you were consuming prior to going on the diet. If, prior to going on the diet, you were drinking two glasses of tea, two cola drinks, and one cup of coffee a day you were consuming about 300 mg of caffeine. You can figure this out more accurately by looking at the caffeine content of various beverages from the previous tables.

Read the label on the No-Doz container or other package you purchased to determine the amount of caffeine in each tablet. Then each day take the number of tablets that will give you an amount of caffeine equal to what you typically drank. Take these tablets for up to a week. It's is a good idea to take the caffeine tablets with food because they make some people nauseated if taken alone. If you are caffeine sensitive you'll begin to react within the week. In other words, the depression you previously experienced will return. If you do experience a resumption of the symptoms, stay away from caffeinated foods and beverages.

After challenging your body with caffeine, then perform a sugar challenge. Eat donuts, pie, cake, cookies, candy or anything else that has sugar in it. I typically use sugar sweetened Kool-Aid because this allows me to exercise greater control over the foods my research participants consume. You only want to find out if you are sugar sensitive so you don't have to be as precise as I do. However, you must make sure that the foods or beverages you consume do not have caffeine—particularly if you found you were caffeine sensitive. This means you must drink caffeine-free sodas if this is one of the means by which you obtain sugar. Similarly, you cannot eat chocolate cake or chocolate pie because they contain caffeine. Remember, during the challenge, you should consume only sugar and not caffeine because we still don't know if they react together.

When challenging your body with sugar, anticipate that the symptoms will return slowly. Some people are very sensitive to sugar, however, and react quickly after consuming only small quantities. Vera was one such individual. When we initiated the sugar challenge, we gave her sugar sweetened Kool-Aid to drink. She called the next day reporting confusion, disorientation, depression, and lack of energy. We asked her to come to the clinic so we could test her to determine the severity of her symptoms. Vera stated she was so disoriented and confused she was afraid to drive. We had to go to her home to test her.

Nancy, on the other hand, was just the opposite. The diet was very effective in eliminating her depression and restoring her energy. However, when we challenged her with sugar sweetened Kool-Aid for six days her depression did not return. She still felt good. But a subsequent interview revealed that if she consumed a large amount of sugar, and this was the primary source of her caloric intake, the depression would return.

Nancy's case is very informative because it demonstrates the interaction that can exist between other foods you eat and the effect of sugar. If you eat a good balanced diet with sufficient protein, the protein can blunt the effect of the sugar. In such an instance the effect of the sugar will be less and, unless you are one of those extremely sensitive individuals, it will take longer for the sugar to have its detrimental impart. Therefore, if you consume sugar for six days and don't feel any worse, reduce your protein intake and increase your sugar intake for another week or two. If you are sugar sensitive, symptoms should now begin to show up.

Will I Always Be Sensitive to Sugar?

The procedure I have just discussed should allow you to identify whether you are sensitive to sugar, caffeine, or both. You may be wondering how you can continue to eliminate these substances when they are so prevalent in our society. Sugar and caffeine are everywhere.

Granted, sugar and caffeine are present in many foods. This means you must get in the habit of reading labels and asking restaurants if they include sugar in foods. Many restaurants will respect your wishes to exclude sugar from the food they serve. Most fast food chains won't, but avoiding such places is a minor concession for feeling good.

As time goes by you will become more adept at spotting substances containing these products. You will also become less and less sensitive, particularly to sugar. This means you can periodically violate the no sugar rule and consume some without harmful consequences. Don't, I repeat, *don't* let this lack of symptoms fool you into thinking you no longer react to sugar. While you may become less and less sensitive the longer you stay off sugar, you are probably still sensitive.

I discussed this issue one evening with a woman whose daughter was sugar sensitive. She stated that her daughter, after being off sugar for some time, tried consuming it again. She was initially delighted to find her symptoms did not return and thought she could continuing eating it with no negative consequences. This was not the case. She soon began to experience a return of the symptoms and realized that she had to again avoid sugar. So the longer you stay off sugar, the less sensitive you are—which means you can consume some without negative consequences. However, don't overdo it. If you do, the symptoms will return.

What About My Cravings for Sweets?

At this point you may be thinking, "How am I going to control my cravings?" Some people have tremendous sugar cravings and believe they can't eliminate it. I fully understand. Sugar cravings can be very strong. The point you must realize is that these cravings will decrease the longer you stay off sugar. I'm not about to state the cravings will totally disappear. For some people they will not, but they will diminish to a point that is tolerable.

What if you give in to the cravings and eat just a little sugar to take the edge off? You can, but you may find this just makes them worse. For some people, all they have to do is consume just a little sugar and the cravings sweep back like a tidal wave. Then they have to exercise tremendous willpower to avoid sugar until the cravings reduce to a manageable level. If you are one of those people with intense sugar cravings, try to stay off sugar. Taking even a little may bring the cravings back in full force.

Caffeine—Can I Ever Drink It Again?

What about caffeine? Does a person's sensitivity to caffeine diminish over time? If your depression is caused by caffeine do you have to stay away from it forever? Yes, I think you do. We seem to become more sensitive to the effects of caffeine as we get older. This is why I believe caffeine responders often cannot identify caffeine as the culprit. A person may have been consuming caffeine for years and only receive the beneficial stimulant effect. Then, as they get older, they become more sensitive. The detrimental effects of caffeine emerge. But because they've been drinking caffeine for years with no negative results they don't suspect this substance.

PART III

MECHANISMS
OF
ACTION

CHAPTER 9

Why Does Sugar Make Me Feel So Bad?

What is it about refined sugar that causes depression? How can it make you tired and moody? Why does it make some people feel bad and not others? These are all very good questions. I just wish I had answers for them.

Several years ago, during a visit to my brother's home, we started discussing psychology (he is a psychologist at UCLA) as we frequently do. During this discussion he made an observation I have always remembered because it is so true. He stated that the easiest task was to describe something like depression. The hardest part was to explain why it occurs. The easiest part, describing depression, was accomplished years ago. The hardest part, explaining *why* the depression occurred, still eludes us.

There are both biochemical and psychological explanations of depression. But neither of these has received complete support. I believe the research I've conducted has taken us a step closer to being able to explain the cause of depression by identifying the influence diet has on it. Although I have identified specific dietary substances—caffeine and sugar—that can produce depression, I've no concrete explanation why they do. There are several possible explanations. In this chapter we'll explore some potential reasons why sugar may cause depression.

Hypoglycemia

Hypoglycemia is a term that literally means low blood sugar. A normal person has a blood sugar level ranging from about 70 milligrams/deciliter of blood to about 110 milligrams/deciliter of blood. A hypoglycemic person experiences a drop in their blood sugar level below about 50 milligrams/deciliter of blood during a test called the oral glucose tolerance test.

In the 1970s a lot of books were written about hypoglycemia. They stated that many psychological and physical disorders could be traced to hypoglycemia and that this disorder was due to eating poor foods—particularly, the consumption of sugar.

Hypoglycemia was apparently considered to be a cause of depression because of the similarity of the symptoms expressed by the hypoglycemic and the depressed individual. A person with hypoglycemia frequently experiences depression. When their blood sugar level falls below 50 milligrams/deciliter of blood, they typically experience depression, fatigue, nervousness, and sleep disturbances. Don't these symptoms sound familiar? They should. These are the same symptoms a depressed person experiences. It used to be assumed that if the same symptoms were experienced by both of these groups of individuals, the underlying cause had to be the same. Because one group was hypoglycemic, it was assumed people with depression were also hypoglycemic.

While this may seem logical, it isn't necessarily true. I identified people seeking psychological counseling who also experienced hypoglycemic-like symptoms, then had these individuals take an oral glucose tolerance test to see if they were hypoglycemic. None of the more than 20 people tested were hypoglycemic. This indicated that hypoglycemia was not the cause of these individuals' psychological problems.

I also reviewed the scientific literature on hypoglycemia and uncovered many other reasons why it was not the cause of most psychological disorders—particular depression. Rather than ask you to believe me, I want to discuss hypoglycemia in more detail.

Categories of Hypoglycemia

Hypoglycemia can be categorized in two ways based on the underlying cause. These two broad categories are *fasting* and *reactive* hypoglycemia.

Fasting hypoglycemia occurs when you fast or go without eating for some time. It is an extremely rare disorder and has many causes, ranging from pancreatic tumors to a metabolic disorder.

Reactive hypoglycemia occurs following the ingestion of food. A person with reactive hypoglycemia will experience a drop in blood sugar level anywhere from two to five hours after drinking a concentrated glucose solution. Reactive hypoglycemia is the most common type.

One variety of reactive hypoglycemia, functional or idiopathic hypoglycemia, accounts for about two-thirds of all cases. This is the type of hypoglycemia most people are talking about when they refer to this disorder. The strange thing is, there is no apparent cause of functional or idiopathic hypoglycemia—no apparent metabolic disorder or any other identifiable problem. There is also no proof that sugar causes it, although it has not been proven that sugar does not cause it either. At the present time we don't know how sugar and functional or idiopathic hypoglycemia are related. It just seems as though many people draw a connection between these two because they both have an impact on blood sugar levels.

Although functional or idiopathic hypoglycemia accounts for most cases of hypoglycemia, it still occurs infrequently. General depression affects about 12 percent of the population at any one time. Functional or idiopathic hypoglycemia occurs much less frequently. Probably less than one-half of one percent of the population have experienced functional or idiopathic hypoglycemia. Therefore, it can only be the cause of depression in less than one-tenth of the cases.

Is Functional Hypoglycemia Even a Disorder?

There are reasons why I question whether functional or idiopathic hypoglycemia should even be considered a disorder. Here is my rationale:

1. True hypoglycemia is always the result of some specific underlying cause. Fasting hypoglycemia, for example, can be caused by a tumor on the pancreas. The tumor causes the pancreas to secrete insulin which in turn causes the cells of the body to use the glucose in the blood stream. If a person does not continue to eat and constantly replenish the blood sugar or glucose, the continued secretion of insulin will cause blood sugar levels to drop.

    In this case, the cause of the low blood sugar level was the pancreatic tumor and its effect on insulin secretion. Hypoglycemia was a symptom of an underlying cause. The true disorder was the pancreatic tumor, not the hypoglycemia. Functional or idiopathic hypoglycemia does not seem to have a specific cause. At least one has not yet been identified.

2. Everyone experiences low blood sugar levels at some point in time. These low blood sugar levels do not produce the symptoms of hypoglycemia in everyone. Studies have been conducted in which a person's blood sugar level has been monitored over a 12 to 24 hour period. As we pass from a fed to a fasted state, our blood sugar level drops into what may be considered a hypoglycemic state. Most of us tolerate this drop quite well and don't even know our blood sugar levels have dropped. If hypoglycemia was truly a disorder, then everyone should experience the symptoms of hypoglycemia because we all experience drops in our blood sugar level.

3. About 25 to 40 percent of the people who take a five-hour oral glucose tolerance test experience a drop in blood sugar levels into what is generally considered a hypoglycemic level. Yet they feel fine. Some individuals have experienced a drop to as low as 25 milligrams/deciliter of blood and remain symptom-free and feeling good. If hypoglycemia was a legitimate disorder these people should have felt bad and experienced a variety of symptoms.

   The implication is that there is not a specific blood sugar level that can be considered diagnostic of a hypoglycemic state. This further clouds the issue. This is something that seems to be very clear in the research literature on hypoglycemia. Some researchers use 50 milligrams/deciliter of blood as the criterion for hypoglycemia, others use 55, yet others 60. There is no one standard level.

4. Studies have revealed that blood sugar levels do not rise as high or fall as low when a person eats a normal meal as they do when people take the oral glucose tolerance test. This suggests that the test for hypoglycemia is not a good one because it does not accurately mimic what happens following normal food consumption.

   Dr. Fred Hofstedt and his colleagues at Fitzsimons Army Medical Center in Aurora, Colorado compared the rise and fall in blood sugar levels when consuming the glucose drink used in the oral glucose tolerance test with the rise and fall in blood sugar levels following ingestion of high sugar content foods such as a piece of pie. These researchers found that normal ingestion of sugar produced much less yo-yoing in blood sugar levels, indicating the oral glucose tolerance test is a poor indicator of what happens following normal food intake.

As you can see, hypoglycemia leaves many unanswered questions. It is because of these difficulties, and the fact that the evidence indicates hypoglycemia is not a cause of depression, that I don't even like to talk about it. I would rather not consider it a disorder. Yet whenever I talk to someone about sugar causing depression or any of the other symptoms like mental confusion, I'm frequently hit with the concept of hypoglycemia.

I recently had a student contact me about her condition. She had been experiencing the classic sugar related symptoms of nervousness, depression, mental confusion, and indecision. She had been to numerous physicians who could not find anything wrong with her. They attributed her problems to some psychological disorder. She was referred to a psychiatrist who placed her on antidepressants, had been hospitalized, and generally battled depression for several years. Then she made an appointment with a doctor who gave her an oral glucose tolerance test.

About 30 minutes after she drank the glucose solution she experienced numerous symptoms. Did her blood sugar level drop to some low level? No! It did not fall much below 60 milligrams/deciliter of blood. Because she felt so bad while taking the test, the physician said she had hypoglycemia and stated that she should eliminate sugar from her diet. She did and began to feel much better.

Note that her blood sugar level did not drop to a level considered to be hypoglycemic. She really didn't have hypoglycemia. Yet she and her physician assumed she did because the sugar brought on her symptoms. Even now she talks about drops in her blood sugar level when she experiences symptoms. This is in spite of the fact that a blood sugar drop did not accompany the appearance of symptoms.

I am not saying this student does not react to sugar. She apparently does. What I am saying is that hypoglycemia was not the cause of her symptoms. We need to get away from the concept of hypoglycemia and direct our attention toward other things that may lead us to the real cause of sugar related symptoms. Now lets get on to other more probable causes of sugar related symptoms.

The Brain's Biochemical Messengers

The most popular explanation of depression and one that has a lot of scientific support, states that depression is due to some abnormality of body chemistry. Depression was originally assumed to have some supernatural or divine origin. This was widely believed by ancient cultures such as Babylonian, Egyptian, and Hebrew. The Old Testament's Book of Samuel stated that King Saul's depression was inflicted by an *evil spirit* sent from God to *torment* him. Job's depression seems to have been the result of the numerous adversities inflicted on him by God to test his faith.

This belief in the supernatural or divine origin of depression disappeared primarily as the result of the teachings of Hippocrates. Hippocrates believed that God would be more likely to purify and sanctify a body than pollute it with something like depression. According to Hippocrates, the brain was the seat of one's mood. When a person experiences depression it is because there is an excessive amount of *black bile,* produced in the spleen or intestine, which corrupts the brain. Although we are not currently attempting to locate and eliminate black bile in depressed individuals, many scientists are convinced that abnormalities in brain chemistry cause depression.

There is evidence to support this assumption. Look at many of the symptoms of depression. Depressed individuals may be agitated and engage in nervous activity such as pacing back and forth or constantly wringing their hands. They may feel so tired they have no energy to do anything and feel like a ton of bricks is tied to their hands and legs. Their mood may change dramatically. Depressed people may experience sleep difficulties, changes in appetite, constipation, inability to concentrate, and a loss of sexual interest. These are changes in bodily function that suggest something physiologically is wrong.

There is also evidence suggesting depression may be due to altered levels of certain chemical substances in the brain. The brain is made up of a large mass of neurons or what might be called nerves. These nerves can be thought of as wires that are connected so information can pass from one part of the brain to another. The important point is that these neurons are not tied together; they don't even touch one another. Instead, there is a small gap between the end of one neuron and the beginning of another as can be seen in figure 9.1.

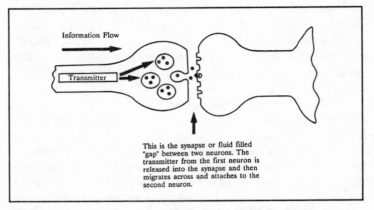

FIGURE 9.1. Illustration of the neurotransmitter of one neuron being released and migrating across and attaching to the second neuron.

The information from one of these neurons is passed to another neuron by a biochemical messenger called a neurotransmitter. These neurotransmitters migrate across and make contact with the next neuron, releasing information. In this way the biochemical messengers play an important role in the normal operation of the brain.

The biochemical theory of depression says that depression sets in when a change occurs in the availability of these neurotransmitters. For example, if the neurons become depleted, information transfer does not take place efficiently and the brain doesn't function normally.

A number of studies have shown that people with depression have altered levels of these neurotransmitters. Several studies have examined the brain of both depressed patients and suicide victims. In both cases there is a decreased level of one specific neurotransmitter.

Antidepressant medications also suggest that neurotransmitters effect depression. Most of these antidepressant drugs act in some way to increase the level of the neurotransmitters.

Diet and Neurotransmitters

At this time you may be thinking, "Okay, I can accept that drugs can have an effect on the brain, but what does that have to do with diet?" This is actually a good question and a very relevant one because this book has focused on diet as a cause of depression. Diet plays a significant role in the regulation of several of the biochemical messengers that have been found to be important in depression.

Two of the most frequently implicated neurotransmitters in depression are serotonin and dopamine. This is important from a dietary perspective because these neurotransmitters are synthesized from two amino acids that we obtain from our diet. Amino acids are the products that make up protein like chicken, fish, and steak.

The two amino acids that seem to be most important for depression are L-tryptophan and tyrosine. They are important because the neurotransmitter serotonin is synthesized from the amino acid L-tryptophan—and the neurotransmitters dopamine and norepinephrine are synthesized from the amino acid tyrosine. This means both serotonin, dopamine, and norepinephrine production are affected by the diet we eat.

Several researchers have even experimented in using these amino acids as drugs in treating depression. These researchers have tried giving each of these amino acids to depressed patients, hoping to eliminate their depression. The results are conflicting. For some people, taking L-tryptophan or tyrosine is of tremendous benefit in eliminating their depression. For others it is not. Some studies have even shown that both of these amino acids must be taken in specific amounts to obtain a continued elimination of depression.

Prior to December of 1989 you could have tried this approach if you had wanted to. However, in November of that year most stores removed L-tryptophan from their shelves because federal health officials reported a link between a mysterious flu-like illness and L-tryptophan. Apparently a large number of people with the symptoms of this illness (high fever, weakness, muscle and joint pain, and swelling of the arms and legs) were taking L-tryptophan. Because so many of these people were taking L-tryptophan, health officials believed this amino acid might be the cause. However, at the time this book is being written, they do not know for sure.

Studies conducted up to this time have led health officials to focus on the way L-tryptophan is made in Japan, the primary source of the supplement. Federal scientists are testing the L-tryptophan tablets remaining in the bottles that people with this illness bought to determine if a contaminant or impurity might have caused the disorder. In other words, right now no one really knows what is causing the illness. This means that, even if you could purchase L-tryptophan, you should avoid it until the cause of the illness is isolated.

Animal studies have revealed that eating sweets produces an increase in the proportion of tryptophan in the blood, relative to a group of amino acids called the large neutral amino acids. As the proportion of available tryptophan increases, the amount that gets into the brain also escalates. This increase results in a boost in the synthesis of serotonin. A number of studies have revealed that the desire for carbohydrates increases as the amount of brain serotonin decreases. Other studies have revealed that depression is associated with a decrease in serotonin. Therefore, the cravings or increased desire for sweets observed in depressed individuals seems to be due to a serotonin deficiency.

While this is a good explanation for a depressed person's increased desire for sweets, it doesn't adequately explain why eliminating sweets helps reduce depression. We know depression is associated with changes in brain chemicals.

And we know the food we eat has an effect on brain chemicals. Just how this complex relationship between the food we eat and the chemicals produced in the brain occurs and is specifically related to depression, is just beginning to unfold. At the present time we have to be content with knowing the food we eat can effect depression and that its effect is probably mediated by altering brain chemicals.

Chromium Deficiency

There is one last mechanism by which sugar may lead to depression. Richard Anderson and his colleagues at the Vitamin and Mineral Nutrition Laboratory, Beltsville Human Nutrition Research Center, have conducted a number of studies revealing that diets high in simple sugars, such as refined sucrose, lead to an increased excretion of chromium.

Chromium is very important because it is involved in normal glucose metabolism or the regulation of blood glucose levels. In fact, chromium is considered so important it has been labeled the Glucose Tolerance Factor.

At the present time the role of chromium in depression is totally speculative. No studies have been conducted investigating the relationship between it and depression. This possible relationship is potentially important, however, because chromium excretion also increases when one is under stress. In another study conducted by Richard Anderson, chromium excretion was measured prior to, and two hours after running a strenuous six-mile stint. Chromium excretion increased nearly five-fold two hours after running. This is valuable data because depression often develops after some stressful event, such as giving birth to a baby or going on a crash diet.

The final piece of evidence comes from a study where Anderson gave eight hypoglycemic patients a chromium supplement. He found the chromium supplementation alleviated their hypoglycemic symptoms. The importance of this study is that many of the symptoms of hypoglycemia are similar to those of depression.

We've seen three possible reasons sugar could cause depression. The hypoglycemic hypothesis is almost certainly wrong. The other two are possible. The neurotransmitter hypothesis seems to have the most validity. However, even this hypothesis is just that—a hypothesis. A tremendous amount of research has been conducted on the role of neurotransmitters in depression and much of this research has been supportive. It has not, however, produced completely convincing evidence that alterations of biochemical messengers are the cause of depression.

Where does this leave us with respect to sugar? I don't know why elimination of sugar results in elimination of depression in sensitive individuals. All I do know is that it does. This is not a totally uncommon situation. There are many instances in which we observe a phenomenon, or can even produce a phenomenon, but don't know exactly why it occurs. For example, we don't know exactly why antidepressants work to eliminate depression in some individuals. This doesn't keep us from using them and getting the benefit from them. The same is true with elimination of refined sugar from the diet. I know it works. It is simple and it is something you can try yourself. Eventually we will identify why it works. In the meantime, you can obtain the benefit and leave it to the scientific community to figure out why it works.

CHAPTER 10

What Does Caffeine Do
and
How Can I Stop Drinking It?

Caffeine is supposed to be a stimulant that increases alertness, but is it also harmful? Why does caffeine make some people depressed and not others? Can caffeine effect me in other ways?

Most of what is known about caffeine is the behavioral effects that occur. For example, it is generally assumed caffeine is a stimulant. Most people drink caffeine to become aroused, to get going. Students drink coffee or take something like No-Doz to stay awake while studying for exams. Many people, as soon as they wake up in the morning, make a pot of coffee. Those who feel a more immediate need for the stimulation of caffeine typically have an automatic coffee maker with a timer device so they don't have to wait for that morning cup of coffee. This practice of drinking coffee in the morning is so much a part of our culture it is almost expected. If you are having breakfast in a restaurant, the waitress will often approach you with a pot of coffee in hand expecting you to want a cup. Some waitresses even act surprised if you don't want coffee.

All of this reinforces the notion that caffeine is a stimulant and that everyone gets a zap from caffeine. However, this is far from true. My wife and I had another couple over for dinner several nights ago and, as frequently happens, part of our conversation focused on my research. Whenever I discuss my research someone always has a personal experience to relate to me. It was no different this evening.

The wife of the couple said she felt better when she eliminated sugar from her diet and the husband stated he could drink several cups of coffee in the evening and go right to sleep. I have no reason to doubt him. However, this statement suggests that the caffeine was not having its presumed stimulant effect. Actually, this is what the research evidence indicates. Research shows that caffeine has many different effects, stimulation is only one of them. When I talk to large groups of people I often illustrate this point by asking three questions:

1. How many of you feel a stimulant effect from drinking caffeine?

2. How many of you do not feel any type of effect from drinking caffeine?

3. How many of you feel worse after drinking caffeine?

A third to a half of the group will raise their hand in response to the first question; about a fourth to a third respond to the second question; and most of the rest of the people will raise their hand in answer to the third question. To further illustrate that caffeine has different effects on different people I ask three more questions.

1. How many of you find caffeine keeps you awake?

2. How many of you find caffeine seems to be a sedative and helps you go to sleep?

3. How many of you find caffeine does not have any effect on your sleep?

Again I find some people in the group respond positively to each of these questions. You might even try this your-self on several of your friends. While this isn't very scien-tific, it indicates that caffeine doesn't have a stimulant effect on everyone. The important point is scientific literature supports this.

Drs. Avram Goldstein and Sophia Kaizer of the Stanford University School of Medicine, Department of Pharmacol-ogy, sent a questionnaire to 250 housewives living in Escondido Village, California. This questionnaire was quite comprehensive and asked them for information about their coffee drinking habits. The questions included such items as:

1. How much coffee do you drink each day?

2. How many years have you been drinking coffee?

3. At what times of the day do you drink coffee?

4. Why do you drink or not drink coffee?

5. How has coffee drinking changed your behavior?

6. How would you be affected if you abstained from morning coffee?

7. Does coffee make you wakeful at night?

This questionnaire was completed by 239 of the house-wives, an excellent response rate. Their replies revealed that different people respond very differently to caffeine. About 25 percent of these housewives said that they did not drink coffee primarily because they didn't like the taste of it. Surprisingly, few of them avoided coffee be-cause of adverse effects such as feeling nervous, shaky, or jittery. Of those who drank coffee, half of them said that caffeine would keep them awake at night if they drank a cup shortly before bedtime; half said it would not. Those who drank the most coffee, especially in the evening, were the ones who believed it had no effect on their sleep.

As you might expect, the questionnaire also revealed that most people drank coffee in the morning—most because they liked the taste and enjoyed it. Many of them stated, however, that they drank coffee because of the stimulant effect it had on them. It helped them *wake up* or *get going*. While these were the most frequently stated reasons, others were also stated, revealing the varied nature of caffeine's effect.

About 20 percent of the coffee drinkers stated caffeine gave them a *feeling of well-being*; another 10 percent said it relaxed them and calmed their nerves. One person even stated that she drank coffee to slow her down. Another stated it made her want to go back to sleep. This person stated that she drank coffee in the evening which is consistent with the apparent sedative effect it seemed to have on her. Such variation in response reflects the different effects which can be produced by caffeine.

Drs. Goldstein and Kaizer then teamed up with a third individual, Dr. Owen Whitby, also at Stanford University. These three researchers conducted a subsequent experiment. They looked at the actual effects of drinking or not drinking coffee in individuals who totally abstained and individuals who were heavy caffeine users, five or more cups of coffee a day. A cup of decaffeinated coffee was prepared for the abstainers and users. Then a vial containing either lactose (milk sugar), 150 or 300 milligrams of caffeine was poured into the coffee they had prepared. The vials were prepared ahead of time so that the research participants did not know what they contained.

After drinking the coffee each person recorded their mood and the way they felt every half hour for the next two hours. This study revealed that abstainers—when they drank the decaffeinated coffee with caffeine added—felt more jittery, nervous, and had an upset stomach. On days when lactose was added to the decaffeinated coffee they felt fine.

This probably explains why abstainers from caffeine state they don't drink coffee. They probably don't like the taste because it is directly linked to the way they feel. After drinking coffee they feel bad, so they connect the coffee drinking to feeling bad and the coffee then takes on the characteristics of feeling bad. This is reflected in the statement, "I don't like the way it tastes."

This analysis of why abstainers don't like the way coffee tastes may sound strange but it's not. Here's why:

There is a psychological phenomenon called *conditioned taste aversion*. This term refers to being conditioned to develop a dislike for some food you ordinarily would like.

This conditioning develops by associating something negative, like feeling bad, with something you've eaten. For example, just about all children like ice cream. Most adults do too. Several years ago it was observed that children with cancer would develop a dislike for ice cream. This seemed very strange, until the phenomena of conditioned taste aversion was applied to the situation.

The cancer stricken children would be required to undergo chemotherapy treatments. For most individuals, chemotherapy is unpleasant and makes you sick. Parents would often try to compensate for this unpleasant experience by giving the child something pleasant like taking them out for ice cream. While the child was eating something desirable, at the same time he or she felt miserable—so the state of feeling bad was associated with the ice cream and led the child to believe he or she didn't like ice cream.

What about heavy caffeine users? When the users drank the decaffeinated coffee with the lactose in it they felt less alert, less active, more sleepy, and more irritable. By the end of the two-hour study period, the users were more jittery, nervous, and shaky than abstainers. Yet when either 150 or 300 milligrams of caffeine was added to the users decaffeinated coffee none of these effects occurred.

This clearly reveals why caffeine users like coffee. It stimulates them. It makes them feel better. When they don't drink it, they feel bad. Clearly, caffeine users are medicating themselves with the most available and frequently used drug in the world. It should also be very clear that caffeine is not just a stimulant. Different people respond very differently to this drug; not everyone receives a stimulant effect.

Caffeine and the Brain

How does caffeine exert its effect? I wish we knew. This doesn't mean we know nothing about caffeine. Caffeine is one of those drugs—yes, I said drug because it is—that does a number of different things within the body. The effects—such as stimulation, anxiety, or making it difficult to sleep—could be produced by one or more of the reactions within the body.

Caffeine is absorbed very easily. It is distributed to virtually every tissue and organ of your body within about five minutes after it is consumed. Maximum blood levels occur within 30 minutes to an hour after consuming caffeine so it is very easily distributed throughout the body.

Once distributed, it starts having its many different effects. They include such things as increasing blood pressure (although this effect may be temporary), altering heart rate, producing cardiac arrhythmias in some people, making it difficult for some people to go to sleep, and making some people nervous and jittery. When these same individuals stop drinking caffeine, they often experience a variety of withdrawal symptoms such as headaches, feeling tired and sleeping more, being anxious, and even some nasal stuffiness.

How can caffeine produce such diverse consequences? Current thinking is that caffeine exerts its effect by influencing the action of a molecule called an adenosine receptor. These receptor molecules are located in a variety of places throughout the body—the brain, the heart, and the kidneys. When they are activated by another molecule called adenosine, a variety of results occur. They include dilating blood vessels which lowers blood pressure and produces sleepiness.

Caffeine has the effect of inhibiting the action of these adenosine receptor molecules. Therefore, when caffeine is consumed the action of the adenosine receptor molecules is inhibited. This means, for example, that the sedation effect of activating the adenosine receptor molecule is blocked. This produces a stimulating effect. Similarly, if dilation of the blood vessels is blocked by caffeine, blood flow is restricted, raising blood pressure.

It is well documented in scientific literature that caffeine inhibits the action of the adenosine receptor molecules. It is also well documented that the action of caffeine is just the opposite of that which occurs from the adenosine receptor molecules. All this supports the notion that caffeine operates by blocking the action of these molecules. However, it is still difficult to explain how caffeine might produce other observed effects such as depression.

Eliminating Caffeine From Your Diet

What if you want to stop drinking caffeine? Lets assume you are one of those people who react to caffeine and want to eliminate it, as did Mary. Mary was referred to me by one of our graduate students, Darren. Darren was conducting a weight reduction study for his dissertation research and had solicited a number of people from the community as research participants. Mary was one of these research participants.

After participating in Darren's study for several weeks, she approached him following completion of the evening's activities. Mary wanted to discuss other problems she was having; she sought advise on how to obtain help for them. From their discussion, Darren found out that Mary had been sexually abused as a child, that she was very moody, had difficulty sleeping, and stayed very angry at her husband. Mary attributed most of this to the sexual abuse she had encountered as a child. This abuse continued to dominate her thoughts almost every day. She was constantly reminded of it from reports on television, reading the newspaper, or virtually anything else.

Darren was aware of my work on diet and depression and thought Mary might profit from my intervention program. The next week he contacted me and we discussed Mary's situation. I thought some of Mary's problems might be diet related and encouraged Darren to refer her to me.

I saw Mary the next week and we discussed her moodiness. She also told me about the abuse she had received as a child and that she was still afraid of males as a result of this. It just so happened that the appointment time we had set up was early in the morning before the clinic actually opened. Mary informed me a sense of fear enveloped her when she realized that she was alone in the clinic with a man and that she didn't feel comfortable being in the same room with me. I told her I understood and that her feelings were reasonable, given the abuse she had encountered as a child. As we discussed her feelings and emotions, I told her that the dietary intervention could help correct many of her emotional problems, such as her moodiness and depression, but she would have to receive some traditional therapy to deal with the sexual abuse she had received.

Mary agreed to try the dietary intervention for two weeks. At the end of that time Mary's sleep problems had disappeared, her depression had lifted, and the anger outbursts she'd always had were now under control. She was very happy with the outcome. As a side benefit, she also found that the sexual abuse she encountered as a child did not bother her as much. While she still needed therapy to resolve this, the diet helped her because now she could control her emotions better. This allowed her to deal more effectively with other facets of her life.

Caffeine was the substance causing Mary's moodiness and depression. When I told her she would have to stop drinking coffee she was initially very hesitant. She consumed the equivalent of about four or five cups of coffee a day and thought she would have trouble giving it up. Fortunately she did not.

When I administer the dietary intervention I ask people like Mary to totally eliminate caffeine. My first approach is to suggest they eliminate it *cold turkey*. At first many people think they can't do this. My reaction is that they should think of this as a temporary event, a short-term change. They are going to eliminate caffeine for only two weeks to see if they will feel better. If they don't, they can resume drinking coffee. Placing a time framework on the intervention seems to be very beneficial for most people. When they develop the mental set that this is only going to last for two weeks, most can eliminate caffeine from their diet.

But for some individuals, even placing such a time limitation is not enough. Earlier, I discussed the withdrawal effects such as headaches that can occur from eliminating caffeine. Some people get such excruciating headaches they can't stop drinking caffeine totally. For these people it is necessary to take a different approach. We gradually wean them off caffeine.

Drs. Richard Foxx and Andrea Rubinoff have investigated a behavioral technique for reducing caffeine consumption among people who consume large amounts of caffeine. The technique they have developed and reported in the *Journal of Applied Behavior Analysis* involves setting progressively diminishing intermediate goals. If you are drinking 10 cups of coffee a day and the goal is to totally eliminate caffeine, then this is the final goal you set.

To reach that final goal you set a series of intermediate goals. During the first week you may set a goal of drinking no more than seven cups of coffee. Each subsequent week you reduce the number of cups of coffee you allow yourself to drink by two or three cups until you reach the final goal of totally eliminating caffeine consumption. In this way you will avoid the severe dilemma of caffeine withdrawal. Even this approach may be difficult for some people. However, it has proven to be effective and can be used by anyone motivated to eliminate caffeine.

CHAPTER 11

Is Caffeine a Health Risk?

Today we live in a health conscious world. Volumes have been written telling us what to eat to live longer and feel better. We are chided to reduce our cholesterol and increase our fiber—all in the name of promoting health.

We're told we need to reduce our caffeine intake. To meet these demands, the beverage industry has come out with decaffeinated soft drinks, decaffeinated tea, and decaffeinated coffee. Drug companies have developed caffeine-free over-the-counter medications. These companies even base some of their advertising campaigns on the fact that their products are caffeine free.

Does this mean caffeine is hazardous to our health? The answer seems to be both yes and no. Caffeine seems to be hazardous to the health of some people, but not others. Remember that caffeine effects different people differently. At the present time most of the research on caffeine is controversial. A general statement cannot be made that will be true for everyone. This doesn't mean that caffeine is *not* hazardous to your health.

Caffeine has been implicated in a variety of both physical and emotional disorders. If you happen to have one of these disorders, caffeine may be the cause, or at least a contributing factor. Or it may have nothing to do with the disorder you are experiencing. If you have one of the disorders that have been related to caffeine I'd recommend you eliminate caffeine consumption.

Emotional Disorders
Related to Depression

Depression

I have talked about depression throughout this book. Most of the research I have focused on has been my own because this is what I'm most familiar with and because my research has focused on treating depression by altering diet. Focusing on my own research may have given you the impression that I am the only person who has found caffeine to be related to depression. This is certainly not the case. Others have also found a connection between depression and caffeine consumption.

Drs. David Veleber and Donald Templer of the California School of Professional Psychology divided a group of 157 volunteers into a low, medium, and high consumption group based on their typical daily use of caffeine. A third of the people in each group were given a cup containing 1 gram of white powder representing some combination of milk sugar (lactose) and either no caffeine, about 200 milligrams of caffeine, or about 400 milligrams of caffeine. Decaffeinated coffee was then added to the cup. Each person completed a psychological test that assessed anxiety, depression, and hostility level prior to—and one hour—after drinking the coffee.

This study found that the level of depression experienced by these individuals one hour after consuming the coffee was related to the amount of caffeine placed in the cup. As the amount of caffeine increased, so did depression. One of the important points of this research is that this study used a group of normal subjects. The increase in depression was not enough to cause concern. It did not approximate a clinical level of depression. But it was enough to detect a change and the change was an increase in moodiness.

Other scientists have focused on the relationship between caffeine and depression in a group of individuals who were emotionally distressed. Drs. John Neil, Jonathan Himmelhoch, Alan Mallinger, Joan Mallinger, and Israel Hanin at Western Psychiatric Institute and Clinic in Pittsburgh assessed the caffeine consumption of a group of depressed individuals receiving treatment at the Affective Disorders Clinic. This study revealed that these depressed individuals were consuming an average of over 400 milligrams of caffeine a day. That is the equivalent of about four cups of coffee or about nine or ten cola drinks. Remember that this is just the average. Some people were consuming a whopping 18 cups a day.

Dr. John Greden and his colleagues at the Clinical Studies Unit, Michigan Medical Center in Ann Arbor, Michigan provided further confirmation that emotionally distressed individuals consume excessive amounts of caffeine—and that as caffeine consumption increases depression also escalates. Dr. Greden assessed the depression level and the amount of caffeine consumed in a group of 83 individuals being treated for a variety of different emotional disorders. These individuals were then divided into a group of high (about seven or more cups of coffee a day), moderate (about two to seven cups of coffee a day), or low (zero to about two cups of coffee a day) caffeine consumers. The depression scores were then related to the amount of caffeine consumed. Again it was found that as caffeine consumption increased so did depression levels.

These are only two of a number of studies that have been conducted. Most indicate the same thing. Unquestionably, caffeine consumption and depression are related. This supports my own research. It does not mean, however, if you experience depression and consume caffeine, that the caffeine is automatically causing the depression. To find out, all you have to do is eliminate the caffeine and see what happens to your depression.

If the depression doesn't go away when you eliminate caffeine, then it is probably due to something else—such as sugar or a situational event like the loss of a loved one. In such a case you may be drinking the caffeine to get a lift and help you out of your depression. The only way you can tell is to experiment with yourself by first eliminating and then reintroducing caffeine into your diet.

Anxiety

Anxiety is a phenomenon that has consistently been associated with caffeine. We have known for many years that caffeine can make a person feel nervous and jittery. In fact, this seems to have been one of the prime factors motivating many companies to produce decaffeinated coffee, tea, and cola products. Advertisement campaigns have even focused on the anxiety producing quality of caffeine in an attempt to promote decaffeinated coffee.

In the typical advertisement we may see a man and a woman conversing and one of them, usually the woman, offers the other a cup of coffee. He declines because he says it makes him nervous and jittery. The woman informs him that it is decaffeinated. Then the man cheerfully and enthusiastically drinks the coffee. The next scene is of the man enjoying the pleasures of the coffee knowing he will not suffer any anxiety because the coffee is decaffeinated.

Studies have documented the anxiety producing effects of caffeine. Drs. Veleber and Templer, in the research I mentioned above, also assessed the relationship between anxiety and caffeine consumption. They found that, as caffeine consumption increased, anxiety levels also mushroomed. This was in a group of normal, nondistressed individuals. Studies have revealed that the anxiety producing effects of caffeine also exist in emotionally distressed individuals.

Drs. Brian De Freitas and George Schwartz at McGill University, Douglas Hospital Centre, were aware of the potential effects of caffeine. They also were aware of the fact that many emotionally distressed patients consume significant amounts of caffeine. It is not uncommon for a distressed patient, while hospitalized, to drink nine or ten cups of coffee a day. To determine the effect of this excessive coffee consumption, the hospital switched from regular coffee to decaffeinated coffee for three weeks. Each hospitalized emotionally distressed patient was assessed on a variety of measures such as anxiety, hostility, and tension prior to the switch to decaffeinated coffee, while they were drinking decaffeinated coffee, and after regular coffee was reinstated. The results of this study revealed that the distressed patients were less anxious, less irritable, and less hostile while on the decaffeinated coffee. And their anxious, irritable, and hostile behavior returned when they started consuming caffeinated coffee once again!

Studies such as these document the anxiety producing effects of caffeine. If caffeine can produce that much anxiety why do people continue to drink it? Many people do stay away from caffeine for just this reason. Some people know if they consume more than a certain amount of caffeine their hand will shake or they will feel nervous and jittery. These people are the fortunate ones. They have identified the cause of their nervousness. Others are not so lucky. They have suffered the anxiety producing effects of caffeine for many years without identifying the cause.

Not too long ago I talked to a woman in her early 20s who constantly felt anxious. One of the manifestations of this anxiety was to bite her finger nails. Her nails were always chewed down to the quick and she couldn't remember the last time she had long fingernails. I told her to try eliminating caffeine from her diet. The next time I saw her, which was several months later, she proudly displayed long fingernails and remarked she was feeling calmer than she had for several months.

These studies and just common sense suggest that anyone with anxiety related problems should eliminate caffeine from their diet to see if it helps them. This common sense suggestion is supported by other studies investigating a specific type of anxiety disorder called a Panic Disorder.

Panic Disorders are characterized by a feeling of impending doom. A person who has a panic attack typically feels like they are dying right then and there. Their heart may start pounding. Their chest can hurt and they may feel dizzy and tremble. During a panic attack a person can have cramps, diarrhea, and nausea. Lights and sounds can seem distorted. Many people think they are having a heart attack or some other serious illness and are rushed to the emergency room.

One of the factors that seems to complicate and possibly induce panic attacks is caffeine. Studies conducted at Yale University School of Medicine and at the National Institute of Mental Health have revealed that individuals who suffer from panic attacks are more sensitive to caffeine. When they consume caffeine they experience symptoms similar to those of a panic attack such as nausea, heart palpitations, restlessness, anxiety, and tremors.

Some panic attack victims have even identified the adverse effect caffeine has on them and have voluntarily eliminated or reduced this substance from their diet. All of this suggests that panic attack victims should totally eliminate caffeine to determine if they feel better when they are caffeine free.

Psychosis

Psychosis is the most severe of the mental disorders. When a person is psychotic he or she loses contact with reality. One of the characteristics of this is hallucinations. A psychotic person may hallucinate, thinking they hear voices or see things that are not there.

There are several examples of excessive caffeine consumption producing a psychotic episode. One such case was reported by Dr. Winston Shen and his colleagues at Charity Hospital in New Orleans. A truck driver had gotten a job at a cola factory. During the month prior to his psychotic episode, his job was to load and unload crates of cola. One of the job's benefits was unlimited access to colas and he apparently took complete advantage of this. On a typical day he'd drink about ten 12-ounce pops. On the day before his hospitalization he more than doubled this cola consumption to 20 to 25 cans. During that day he progressively felt more and more uneasy.

The next day he complained his *nerves were bad* and started having visual hallucinations. He began seeing bright shiny flies and bugs that supposedly were attacking and biting him. The flies and bugs were supposedly controlled by *voodoo* and he was constantly shouting for people to get the flies off of him. In addition to this hallucination he believed someone was pouring gasoline on him. This individual had lost contact with reality. There were no flies or bugs and no one was trying harm him.

After being admitted to the hospital, the truck driver was given a variety of examinations all of which were negative. There was nothing wrong with him that could be detected. The only conclusion they could reach was that he had *flipped out* from excessive caffeine consumption.

The hospital staff continued to observe him for the next week. No changes were seen in his behavior for the first 24 hours. At the end of the second day the hallucinations had disappeared and he continued to improve over the next week. By the end of the week his mental state was back to normal.

This example is an extreme illustration of the effect of excessive caffeine consumption. A psychotic state such as that produced in the truck driver is rare, but it does occur. I am including it not to scare you, but to illustrate the many and diverse effects caffeine can provoke.

The case of the truck driver also illustrates the length of time that may be needed to recover from the effects of caffeine. This person took a whole week to get back to normal. While most people do not need this much time, they do need more then several hours to totally recover and eliminate caffeine from their system.

Sleep

One consistent finding with regard to caffeine is its effect on sleep—and I don't mean it helps you fall asleep! This is something I can really relate to because caffeine has a very negative effect on my sleep. About a year ago I had gradually developed the habit of drinking a cola in the morning and afternoon while writing papers, counseling students, or preparing lectures. I also would frequently drink a glass or two of tea at lunch time so I was consuming about 150 milligrams of caffeine a day. This is not very much. However, I am apparently very sensitive to caffeine.

Shortly after I started drinking this much caffeine I began having some difficulty falling asleep and after I was asleep I would wake up several times during the night. In general, I had difficulty sleeping. If my wife got up during the night I would, at times, think she woke me up. At other times I couldn't blame her for my insomnia.

This went on for several months until I thought about caffeine. "Maybe caffeine is destroying my sleep," I reasoned. I don't remember any time in which I had consumed this much caffeine, so I decided to eliminate it from my diet. Within a few days my sleep returned to normal. Since that time I almost totally avoid caffeine.

This effect of caffeine on sleep is not unique to me. Many good research studies have documented the negative effect caffeine has on sleep. Vlasta Brezinova conducted a study at the sleep laboratory, University of Edinburgh, Edinburgh, Scotland several years ago. It essentially revealed the same thing I experienced. Brezinova found that individuals who drank a cup of decaffeinated coffee with 300 milligrams of caffeine in it slept much less during the night, took longer to fall asleep, and awakened more frequently during the evening than when they drank a cup of decaffeinated coffee.

This is just one of many studies that have documented this effect. Remember though, everyone's sleep is not affected by caffeine. Some people can drink a cup of coffee, fall asleep immediately, and slumber soundly. Once again, this indicates the individual differences in the effect of caffeine. If you are sleeping soundly and fall asleep immediately, then caffeine is probably having little if any effect on your sleep. If, however, you are troubled by insomnia, try eliminating caffeine. It may be your problem.

Physical Disorders Related to Caffeine

In addition to the emotional and behavioral disorders I just discussed there are a variety of physical disorders that have been related to caffeine. Generally they are more serious because they may represent the result of continuous consumption of caffeine over a longer period of time. These conditions do not seem to be reversed as readily by eliminating caffeine.

Before I present these physical disorders I want to caution you that there is controversy over caffeine's contribution. Some researchers are adamant, certain that caffeine contributes to each of these disorders; others question caffeine's role. Given this controversy what should you do? My suggestion is to eliminate caffeine from your diet if you have one of these disorders. This certainly won't hurt you and it may help.

Fibrocystic Breast Disease

Fibrocystic breast disease is a benign or noncancerous disorder that can be loosely defined as a condition in which the breasts are lumpy and sore. It is important to realize that all women whose breasts are occasionally lumpy and sore do not have fibrocystic breast disease. And not all breast lumps are fibrocysts. Only your physician can make this diagnosis.

About 10 years ago an article appeared in the *American Journal of Obstetrics and Gynecology* suggesting that caffeine may be important in the development of fibrocystic breast disease. Later that year another study was published in a journal called *Surgery* that compared the breast lumps and soreness of women with fibrocystic breast disease who eliminated caffeine for eight weeks with a group of women who continued to consume caffeine. This study reported that the women who discontinued caffeine experienced a decrease in soreness and lumps.

The results of this study are potentially very important because of the tremendous implications they have for many women. One of the problems with this study is that the researchers and the women knew who stopped and who continued drinking caffeine. This raises the possibility of an unconscious bias. The women who stopped drinking coffee may have expected less soreness in their breasts and this expectation may have caused them to think they were not as sore.

A number of other studies were conducted that attempted to eliminate this bias to determine if caffeine is actually related to fibrocystic breast disease. A 1986 report published in the *Archives of Internal Medicine* summarized the studies published up to that time. This report revealed that some of these studies found a relationship but most did not.

So what is the effect of caffeine on fibrocystic breast disease? We still don't know the answer. Maybe caffeine is related to fibrocystic breast disease or maybe there is a relationship in only a small group of women with this problem. Because we don't know for certain, I would recommend eliminating caffeine and see if you feel a reduction in soreness and lumps. If you do, great, even if this reduction is due to something other than caffeine. Stay away from caffeine.

Although we don't know for certain if caffeine causes fibrocystic breast disease, women consistently report a decrease in tenderness of their breasts when they eliminate caffeine. I know of several women who report this. These same women state that their breasts become sore when they start drinking caffeinated beverages again. These women don't care if this is *unscientific*. They feel the effect and stay off caffeine for that reason. If you suffer from this disease, the only way you can tell if caffeine is a problem is to eliminate it for several weeks, and then start drinking it again. If you get relief when you are off caffeine and the soreness returns when you resume it, you're are probably sensitive to caffeine and need to avoid it.

Coronary Heart Disease

Loosely defined, coronary heart disease refers to having a heart attack. This is obviously something very serious everyone would like to avoid.

One of the most alarming studies on caffeine as a health risk appeared about a decade ago in the prestigious *New England Journal of Medicine*. This study compared the coffee consumption of a group patients who had just had a heart attack with patients who were hospitalized for other reasons. It found that the heart attack patients not only consumed more coffee but were about twice as likely to have a heart attack if they drank six or more cups of coffee a day.

This finding was consistent with others' suspicions. Coffee consumption had been suspect for some time because caffeine has a number of effects, such as altering one's heart rate, temporarily increasing blood pressure, and boosting cholesterol levels—which increase the risk of having an attack. Therefore, a study that found a relationship between coffee consumption and heart attacks was critical. But it needed to be confirmed by subsequent research. These subsequent studies clouded the picture rather than clarifying it. Some of them found a relationship with coffee consumption; others did not.

In 1986 a report was published in the *New England Journal of Medicine* that seemed to clarify the confusion created by prior studies. This study measured the amount of coffee consumed 10 years, 5 years and less than 5 years prior to having a heart attack. The relationship between having a heart attack and the amount of coffee consumed was then computed for each of these time periods. It was found that the strongest association between coffee consumption and having a heart attack existed when the amount of coffee consumed was measured right before the heart attack. The risk of having a heart attack was two to three times higher for individuals drinking five or more cups of coffee right before the heart attack occurred. When coffee consumption was measured 10 or more years before the heart attack, no association was found.

This finding should not have come as much of a surprise. Caffeine has an acute effect on people. The effect of caffeine is immediate and does not seem to build up over time as does smoking. Caffeine's effect on blood pressure is a good example of this. When you drink caffeine your blood pressure rises. If you stop drinking caffeine the effect on blood pressure goes away. So whatever effect caffeine is going to have will occur rather rapidly without any cumulative power. This means that, if you are at risk for having a heart attack you should stay away from caffeine or at least reduce your consumption to about two cups of coffee, four cola drinks, or four glasses of tea.

Cholesterol

Practically all the experts are telling us to cut back on foods high in cholesterol. The poultry and fish industries have capitalized on this very effectively, much to the dismay of the beef industry. For years researchers concentrated on producing tender meat. They successfully accomplished this by creating a *marbling* effect. This marbling was nothing more than increasing the saturated fats in the meat, which made it more tender. The problem is that these saturated fats also contributed to increased cholesterol levels.

The media has warned the public about the danger of eating too much of this tender marbled beef. And the public responded by switching to more poultry and fish. Now, in the interest of reducing cholesterol, the beef industry is trying to produce a leaner cut of meat with less saturated fat.

What about caffeine? It has been known for years that caffeine consumption increases the free fatty acids in the blood stream. How does that impact cholesterol? This has been the subject of some controversy. Some of the initial studies did not find an association between coffee consumption and cholesterol level. However, several of the more recent studies have. For example, a report published in the 1986 issue of the *American Journal of Epidemiology* compared the serum cholesterol levels of about 6,000 men consuming various levels of caffeine. This report found that those individuals consuming no caffeine had the lowest cholesterol levels. As caffeine consumption increased serum cholesterol levels also rose.

This finding is somewhat consistent with a report published in the 1985 issue of the *American Journal of Epidemiology*. The only problem is that the 1985 report found a relationship only with women, whereas the 1986 report focused only on men and found a relationship. The apparent conflict between the two reports may be because the 1985 report studied only 320 men whereas the 1986 report studied about 6,000 men, thus giving a better opportunity to detect a relationship.

What does this say about cholesterol and caffeine? It indicates that caffeine can increase your cholesterol levels. If you drink caffeine, particularly if you drink five or more cups of coffee a day and have a high cholesterol level, you should consider eliminating caffeine—or at least reducing your intake and see what effect it has on your cholesterol levels.

One of the research participants who was involved in one of my studies returned after being on the diet two weeks and elatedly proclaimed that his cholesterol level had dropped. This person was a biochemistry major, knew he had high cholesterol levels, and periodically checked them because he had access to all the necessary equipment.

What implications does this have for you? I think they are quite clear. If you have high cholesterol levels and also drink a significant amount of caffeine, eliminate the caffeine for several weeks and then get your cholesterol level checked again. You might be pleasantly surprised. You could even try this if you consume only a moderate amount of caffeine because, for some individuals, even small amounts can have significant effects.

Before I leave this section I want to emphasize that you should not assume that caffeine is the total culprit or that elimination of it is the cure for high cholesterol. If only it were that simple! In some cases it may be. In other cases, although elimination of caffeine may help reduce your high cholesterol levels, you may have to watch your overall cholesterol intake and even use some medication to control it. As always, you should discuss this with your physician.

PART IV

HOW TO TELL
IF YOU
ARE DEPRESSED

CHAPTER 12

Symptoms of Depression

Patty, a vivacious, eighteen-year-old, had been going with Jim for about a year. Jim was madly in love with her and frequently brought up the topic of marriage. Although Patty had strong feelings for him, they were not as strong as his. Patty also realized she did not want to seriously consider marriage until she had finished college. To further complicate matters, she and Jim would be attending different schools for at least three years. During Patty's first year of college she and Jim attended the same university and were together almost all the time. While they did have many arguments and difficult times, these tended to be short lived and were resolved rather quickly.

After finishing her first year of college Patty knew that she would have to attend another university several hundred miles away because she was majoring in nursing and that university offered the best program. Although Jim initially found it very difficult to accept the fact she would be leaving in September, he finally did.

When Patty left for college Jim gave her a big parting kiss with the assurance that they would call each other at least twice each week and that Patty would come home every second or third weekend. During the first few months everything proceeded as scheduled. She called Jim every Tuesday evening and he called her every Thursday evening. Whenever Patty came home they were together most of the time. On one of these trips home, Jim even gave Patty a promise ring apparently solidifying their commitment to each other.

But Patty wasn't as committed to the relationship as was Jim. She enjoyed socializing much more than he did. Over time she met other young men and started going out with them. This made her realize she was too young to make the commitment Jim wanted, so she broke off the relationship.

Jim was devastated. He moped around the house feeling numb. Jim would sit in a chair looking into space for hours or go to his room and just lie there gazing at the ceiling. At times he would fall asleep. When he awoke he didn't feel any better. He was depressed and had no energy. At night, sleep didn't come easily. Patty was always on his mind. He would even wake up in the middle of the night thinking about her.

When his mother called him for dinner he didn't want to eat because he wasn't hungry. When he did go down for a meal he would just stare at the food and leave most of it on his plate. During the next week he lost over five pounds. On Saturday night he went out with friends. At one of the local fast food places they met a group of girls. Jim tried to act interested but he didn't care about trying to pick up one of them. All he could do was think of Patty.

When he and the guys went out the next weekend, however, a cute little brunette caught his eye. She wasn't as lively as Patty, but he enjoyed her company.

Dorothy, an only child, grew up in a home filled with constant bickering. Her mother always complained about her father—and with good reason. He was an alcoholic and was very abusive to both Dorothy and her mother. Dorothy gradually learned to hate her father so much she could not look him in the face. This turmoil at home was so great she rushed into marriage when she was 18 to escape her intolerable home situation.

Dorothy's husband was a devoted man who was always patient and understanding, even though she was often angry and irritable with him. He gave her the moral support to cope with everyday problems which helped Dorothy immensely.

When Dorothy's husband was 42-years-old he developed a gastric ulcer and had to follow a strict diet to keep it under control. Even though he followed this diet carefully he was hospitalized three times for bleeding ulcers. He died suddenly of a blood clot several days after his third admission to the hospital. Dorothy's husband's death was very traumatic for her. Month's later she still suffered from insomnia and intense headaches. She felt totally alone. Then her daughter married and moved to another part of the city and her son began preparing to go away to college. These events made her feel like she was being totally abandoned.

Dorothy was also afraid she could not afford to send her son to college, so she found a job as an office clerk. Although the job was fine and something she could handle, Dorothy had difficulty getting along with the other people in the office. She liked to do things her way and not take directions from the boss. She would even try to tell others how to do their job if she thought they were performing in an inefficient manner. This did not make for good relations with co-workers and even resulted in a reprimand from her superior. Dorothy solved this problem by not paying attention to others in the office and developing only superficial relationships with them.

Although she reached some solution with her job, she felt that she never recovered from the shock and grief of her husband's death. During the following year she became increasingly nervous and finally made an appointment with her family physician, who gave her medication to calm her down.

The medication helped some. But over time Dorothy became increasingly anxious, agitated, and depressed. She was unable to sleep, afraid of the future and what it held for her. She believed all of her difficulties would not have existed if her husband were still alive. She had developed strong guilt feelings about his death because she was convinced her anger and their arguments had killed him.

Over the next twenty years Dorothy's symptoms became increasingly worse. She became excessively sensitive to noises. It was just about impossible for her to make decisions even about little things. And she was bothered about all the changes taking place in her life. Depression set in and Dorothy continually felt her life was empty and meaningless. For a six-year period she was placed on antidepressant medication which helped some but did not totally eliminate the depression or the empty feeling and guilt she harbored. She quit taking the medication and functioned somewhat effectively for four years. But then the depression, agitation, and sleeplessness returned. Dorothy started taking antidepressants again and was able to function a little better.

At age 62 she began deteriorating even further. She quit her job because she was making more and more mistakes. Her inability to make decisions got worse because she was afraid she would make a bad or wrong decision. She constantly complained about fatigue, poor appetite, and chronic constipation. She had frequent crying spells and at times felt as though her whole body was trembling. She would wake up at four in the morning and couldn't fall asleep again. Dorothy wished she were older so she would die and her misery would be over.

Jim and Dorothy were both experiencing depression. However, there is a big difference in the level and severity of their depression. Jim's depression was a normal expression of the termination of a relationship that meant a great deal to him.

There are times when it is natural to feel depressed. Our moods do not remain the same day after day. We experience elation when we do something good or when something pleasant happens to us such as winning a prize, doing well on an examination, or seeing someone we love for the first time in several years. We experience various degrees of depression when bad things happen to us.

Failing an exam, having a relationship terminated as was Jim's, or the death of a loved one such as Dorothy experienced are all traumatic.

The difference between Jim and Dorothy is that Dorothy's depression seemed to have roots in her earlier life and the loss of her husband merely served to accentuate a condition that already existed. Dorothy did not get over the loss of her husband. Instead, her depression continued to get worse and persisted for many years whereas Jim's ran a normal course.

Identifying Serious Depression

How can you distinguish between a level of depression that does not require professional help and one that does? This is a very important and serious question because the language used by a person with a normal level of depression and one with severe depression requiring professional help may be very similar.

Look at the symptoms experienced by both Jim and Dorothy. They both felt low and depressed. They both lost their appetite, could not sleep, had difficulty in concentrating and lost interest in many of life's pleasures. If you look at the symptoms they were experiencing there is virtually no difference between these two. There is also little difference in the self descriptions of a person experiencing depression that does not require professional help and one that does. Both of these people would describe themselves as feelings blue, sad, unhappy, empty, low, or lonely.

Although the self descriptions and the symptoms of people with different levels of depression are similar, people who have experienced both levels of depression state that their *feelings* during clinical depression are very distinct from any feeling they had during a normal low time. It is just that this difference is difficult to communicate. In both cases symptoms such as fatigue are common, but the subjective experience of fatigue is different. This is the difficult thing to express.

Symptoms of Depression

The symptoms Dorothy and Jim were experiencing should give you some idea of the numerous and varied characteristics of depression. Aaron Beck, a psychiatrist at the University of Pennsylvania and one of the country's leading depression researchers, has categorized the symptoms of depression in the following way.

Emotional Manifestations

Emotional manifestations refer to a person's feelings. It refers to the way a person feels or to the changes that occur in their actions as a direct result of their feelings. The feelings that are included under the heading of emotional manifestations are as follows:

1. *Dejected Mood* — A dejected mood refers to feeling sad or unhappy. A depressed person typically describes the way they feel with words like miserable, hopeless, blue, sad, lonely, unhappy, humiliated, ashamed, worried, useless, or guilty.

   A person with only a mild level of depression will typically say they feel sad or blue but the feeling fluctuates during the day. These sad or blue feeling can be relieved or eliminated by hearing a joke or getting a compliment. As a person becomes more severely depressed the sad and blue feelings are more difficult to eliminate. Now a joke or a compliment has little if any effect. If it does have an effect it does not last long. When a person is severely depressed he or she feels miserable, hopeless, and sad all the time. It doesn't make any difference what others do. Virtually nothing can cheer up a severely depressed individual.

2. *Negative Feelings Toward Self* — A depressed person tends to not like him or herself and may feel worthless. A person with a mild case of depression may feel disappointed in him or herself and as though they have let everyone down. Such a feeling exists in many students after they have failed a class or flunked out of school. In the more extreme case, the depressed person feels

as though they can't do anything right, that they are no good. They may even think they are so terrible they have no right to live or that they are despicable.

3. *Reduction in Gratification* — A person who is depressed gets very little gratification or satisfaction from their work, their friends, eating out, going to parties or even from taking a vacation.

A mildly depressed person will typically report they no longer get a *kick* out of their job, friends, or family or that something that they previously enjoyed, such as fishing or playing racquetball, is no longer fun. Instead, they find passive activities such as watching television or reading a book are more enjoyable.

As depression becomes more severe, apparent boredom sets in and activities such as watching a good football game are no longer exciting. In the extreme case it doesn't make any difference what the individual does. Nothing is enjoyable or exciting.

4. *Loss of Emotional Attachments* — A depressed person often loses affection or concern for people who should mean the most to them — such as their spouse, their children, or their parents.

In cases of mild depression a person might feel their love or affection for these family members has decreased. As depression gets worse the loss becomes more acute. Now a depressed person's concern for a spouse, their children, their parents, or a job no longer exists. They may reach the point where they don't care what happens to them. They may even feel as though they hate their family.

The loss of emotional attachment can even affect the depressed person's concern with their own appearance. They may not comb their hair or iron their clothes. I had one client who told me she had deteriorated to the point she didn't care how she looked.

5. *Crying Spells* — One very common symptom of depression is the ease and frequency of crying. This is more common among women than among men. Situations that

ordinarily would not elicit tears now do. Often a depressed person feels they have no control over their crying. Just about anything can trigger a crying spell. One of my clients could not tell me how she felt without crying. Regardless of how hard she tried, she couldn't hold back the tears. She cried for no reason at all.

6. *Loss of Sense of Humor*—A person does not have much of a sense of humor when they are depressed. The depressed person is not amused and does not feel like laughing at a jesting remark, a joke or cartoon. They do not handle kidding well or joshing by their friends. Kidding that would have been seen as humorous at one time no longer is humorous and may even be seen by a depressed person as an insensitive, cruel remark. A depressed person cannot see the light side of friendly kidding. He or she tends to take everything seriously. In the seriously depressed person a joke or kidding remark is likely to result in an aggressive or hostile reply and cause the depressed person to feel hurt or disgusted.

Cognitive Manifestations

Cognitive manifestations refer to a person's beliefs and attitudes about him or herself. A depressed person tends to have very negative attitudes and thoughts about him or herself. These beliefs, thoughts, and attitudes include the following:

1. *Low self-esteem*—Depression is marked by low self-esteem. A depressed person tends to view him or herself as inadequate in virtually all respects. They see themselves as sickly, dumb, weak, not popular, and unattractive.

In cases of mild depression a person overreacts to difficulties such as not getting hired for a job or making a bad grade. As depression becomes more severe these thoughts become increasingly self destructive and the past, present, and future are viewed as being a failure.

Take a look at John's situation. He had just failed a test. This makes him start thinking that he had done poorly throughout his academic career and will continue to fail if he remains in school.

In the severe case the person views the self as a total failure; as worthless and completely inept as a student, parent, employee, etc. Many times depression causes one to believe they are a burden to their friends and family and that these people would be better off without them.

2. *Gloomy and pessimistic outlook on life*—In addition to having low self-esteem, a depressed person has a gloomy and pessimistic outlook on life and a general feeling of hopelessness. Depression causes one to view the future in terms of the present. For example, Sally was despondent and having some serious difficulties with her boyfriend. She couldn't see how anything could make things better between the two of them. Any time someone would make a suggestion about how to make things better, Sally would come up with some reason why it wouldn't work.

This very gloomy and hopeless view causes the depressed person to perceive the future as black and hopeless and to believe that things cannot get better. Therefore, a depressed person either feels like they won't like something, it won't do any good, or they know that things won't get any better.

Friends, family, and others who try to help the depressed person get very frustrated with this outlook. Sometimes family and friends get so tired of this negative outlook they throw up their hands in defeat.

This negative outlook can even cause a depressed person to discard their antidepressant medication. I knew of one individual who tried to commit suicide by taking an overdose of the antidepressants that had been prescribed for his depression.

This gloomy outlook on life and the low self-esteem cause the depressed person to criticize and blame themselves for all their seeming deficiencies. This tendency is compounded by the fact that rigid, perfectionistic standards are set that cannot be met. A student may berate him or herself and think they are dumb or stupid if they don't get all *A's* or if they have to study a little harder to get the same grades as their roommate. Another person may think they can't keep friends if they get into a fight or argument with someone they think highly of. It is very difficult for a depressed person to accept the fact that it is human to err and that every problem or difficulty is not their fault.

3. *Inability to make decisions* — The depressed person has difficulty making decisions and frequently changes their mind. This can be very trying to family and friends. They question "Why can't you make up your mind?" This type of statement can cause a depressed person to start crying and say, "You don't understand." Such comments are viewed as cruel and unkind.

   There are actually two kinds of indecisiveness characteristic of depression. One form comes from being afraid of making the wrong decision. I know a client who actually stated she was afraid to make a decision because she was afraid it would be wrong. The depressed person has no confidence in their ability to make a good decision.

   The other form of indecisiveness comes from knowing that if a decision is made, they will have to start a course of action. Remember that one of the characteristics of depression is fatigue and lack of motivation. If a decision is not reached then nothing has to be done. If a decision is reached, then you have to start doing something. It is similar to the person who couldn't see any pleasure in taking a trip to Europe because of the work required in preparing for the trip. Similarly, if a housewife can't decide on what to fix for supper, she doesn't have to get up and fix anything.

4. *Distortion of body image* — A final cognitive manifestation of depression is a distortion of body image. Depression frequently causes a person to believe they are unattractive. A woman may carefully examine her face for blemishes or wrinkles. She may also be preoccupied

with becoming fat. One rather severely depressed client I worked with had, several years earlier, maintained a very rigid diet in which she ate only at specific times during the day and then would allow herself to eat for only a certain amount of time, such as five minutes. Every calorie was counted to make sure she was not eating too much. By the time she received help she weighted only 94 pounds. She was 5 feet, 6 inches tall—so this was definitely not her normal weight.

Motivational Manifestations

1. *Loss of Motivation*—One of the characteristic features of depression is a preference for passive activities such as watching television. Avoiding active activities, such as dancing or hiking, reflects a decline in motivation. In the extreme case, this loss of motivation may extend to performing even the most vital tasks such as eating, or taking medication to relieve the depression. Family and friends can urge, cajole, or even threaten the depressed person—but it does little good. They still do as little as possible.

When depression is mild this lack of motivation is generally manifested by feeling a loss of interest or drive to do things that were previously interesting and a challenge. For example, I know a housewife who, prior to becoming depressed, volunteered for community and service projects. At home she kept her house spotless and always prepared wonderful meals. During her depressed state she lost her desire to do anything. Meals consisted of preparing whatever was quick and easy and she stopped all of her community involvement. She had no desire to do anything. According to her, she just did things mechanically without any feeling. She felt like she was a robot. When she ran down and could do no more, she just stopped.

In more severe cases the depressed person does so little they perform essentials like brushing their teeth only with extreme effort and only when *forced* to do it. A dentist told a depressed man to brush his teeth three or four times a day. "Three or four times!" the man complained. "It takes all the energy I have to brush once."

This lack of motivation is also seen in the depressed person's desire to escape from or break their daily routine. A depressed individual typically thinks all their problems would be solved if they could just get away or get out of their lousy current situation. A housewife may yearn to get away from her children or get a job and escape the boring, meaningless life she is leading. A college professor described his escapist feeling as wanting to be in almost any other occupation than teaching. When he would ride the bus to work he would wish that he were a bus driver rather than a professor.

These dreams of escape or diversion constantly enter the depressive's thoughts. They daydream of changing jobs, going to a movie, or becoming a hobo. As the depression becomes more severe the depressed individual may even withdraw from social contacts because being nice and polite is too demanding. One of my clients told me that, while on a vacation, she stayed in her room and slept because she could not take all the noise of being around others and didn't feel like engaging in *happy chatter.* This doesn't mean that the depressed person doesn't want to be with other people. They may desire company but it is just too demanding.

2. *Suicidal thoughts*—Suicidal thoughts are also very characteristic of depression. In less severe cases of depression a person will tend to think they would be better off dead or they find the idea of dying attractive. As depression becomes worse the suicidal thoughts are more compelling and frequent—and the risk of either an impulsive or premeditated suicidal attempt increases.

As depression becomes more severe, a more definite desire to die develops. The depressed person may believe their family and friends would be better off if they were dead. At times this desire to die may be manifested by taking unnecessary risks. A college professor I knew broke his arm and, just after having the cast removed, swam across a swift, treacherous river hoping he couldn't make it and would drown. He actually bragged about this foolish attempt. Unfortunately, no one believed he was actually attempting suicide until he shot himself in the head about a week later.

Physical Manifestations

The physical manifestations of depression appear in a variety of areas. A depressed person can lose their appetite, experience a sleep disturbance, lose their sex drive and develop fatigue.

1. *Loss of appetite*—For many individuals, this represents one of the first signs of depression, although some people have an increase in appetite when they get morose. When depression effects appetite, it initially takes the form of meals no longer tasting good or that the depressed person doesn't enjoy food like he or she use to. As the depression gets worse a depressed person may skip meals and even show a dislike for food.

2. *Sleep disturbance*—In addition to losing their appetite, sleep becomes more difficult. Some individuals wake up earlier than usual and can't go back to sleep—not because they've had enough sleep, but because they can't fall asleep again.

   Others sleep much more than usual. They may sleep 10 or 12 hours a night and still feel as though they need more rest. Still others may go to sleep quickly but wake up at two or three in the morning. Frequently a depressed person claims, "I haven't slept all night." While this is seldom true, this is the way they feel.

3. *Loss of sexual desire*—Depression also manifests itself in terms of a loss of sexual drive. A mildly depressed individual may lose their spontaneous desire for sex. However, with a little effort their partner can arouse them. In more extreme cases of depression sexual desire is markedly reduced and a person can be aroused only with considerable stimulation.

4. *Fatigue*—One of the more prominent features of depression is a constant complaint of fatigue. The fatigue they are complaining about is not the same as having just completed a hard day's work. The depressed individual would love to experience that kind of tiredness. The fatigue that is experienced is more debilitating and unpleasant. Their arms, legs, or even their entire body may feel heavy—as though it is weighted down with lead. This fatigue causes the person to feel totally worn out and run down. Although fatigue is a prominent factor, rest and sleep do not help. A depressed individual can sleep for 8 or 10 hours a night, take naps, and still feel fatigued.

These physical symptoms of headache, fatigue, loss of appetite and sexual desire, and sleep disturbances represent the primary complaint of most depressed individuals. They are the symptoms for which these people tend to seek help. Some depressed individuals even have CAT scans to check for tumors as possible causes of their headaches. Frequently, the attending physician will attempt to treat the physical complaint instead of questioning the patient to see if the physical complaint is part of a more overall problem such as depression. Treatment of the complaints can continue for years before it is recognized that this is just one manifestation of the underlying depression.

Jane is a good example of such a case. An attractive woman in her 50s, Jane had been complaining about sleep difficulties, headaches, anxiety, nervousness, and fatigue for over a decade. When I met her the first time she was taking a double handful of drugs to treat each of these symptoms, as well as several others. Never once did any of her doctors suggest she might be suffering from depression or refer her to a mental health professional.

When I started questioning her I found that, in addition to all the physical problems she was having, she also cried all the time, felt worthless and down in the dumps, was moody, and always irritated with her husband. Jane's primary problem was depression. The numerous symptoms she was experiencing were all tied to it. Once the cause of the depression was eliminated, her fatigue, sleep difficulties, headaches, crying spells, moodiness, and irritability all disappeared.

If you are one of those individuals who has some of these symptoms, does this mean you are depressed and need the help of a mental health professional? Perhaps. Perhaps not. In the next chapter I'll give you some guidelines that will help you decide if your symptoms are a natural fluctuation in mood which we all experience from time to time—or if your symptoms suggest something more serious.

CHAPTER 13

Normal Blues
or Clinical Depression

As we've learned, depression is characterized by physical symptoms such as an inability to sleep well and constant fatigue, as well as by psychological symptoms such as a low self-esteem. In general, a depressed person feels bad all the time. When is this feeling something that can be considered a normal low and when is it serious enough to warrant professional help?

We all have fluctuations in mood. Sometimes you feel good and on top of the world. Everything is rosy and wonderful. Other times things are so-so—not bad, but then again, not real good either. There are yet other times when you feel really down in the dumps. You can't sleep even though you're tired, you have no appetite, you don't want to do anything, nothing interests you. When you feel like this you are depressed. When are these symptoms an indication of something serious—and when are they a normal fluctuation in mood or a normal reaction to something bad that has happened to you and nothing to worry about? Before trying to help you answer this question, go back over the symptoms presented in the last chapter and ask yourself, "Is this characteristic of me?" Do you have a number of these symptoms?

Any person can experience one or more of the symptoms for reasons other than depression. For example, a headache can be caused by tension. Similarly, fatigue can be the result of an insufficiently functioning thyroid gland.

If you have a few of the physical symptoms it is important to determine if there is an underlying physical cause. This means that you must make an appointment with your physician and have him check you for the presence of some physical disorder.

If you have a number of these symptoms and many of them are the emotional, cognitive, and motivational symptoms such as feeling sad or unhappy, crying easily, lack of motivation, and constant fatigue—you are probably depressed. Treating one or two of the more prominent physical symptoms will not make you feel as good as you want to feel.

This is not to say that a physical problem could not cause all these symptoms. It could. That's why it is important for you to have your physician check them out. If he or she can't find anything wrong with you, however, giving you a pill for your headache or your anxiety will do little to help you feel as good as you want to feel. If you continue to be lethargic and moody even though you are taking the medication your physician prescribes—and tests indicate you are healthy—it's time to consider depression.

How Serious Is Your Depression?

Lets assume you have gone through the last chapter and found you do indeed have many of the symptoms discussed. You have also made an appointment with your physician and had a thorough check-up. You were given a clean bill of health. What now?

First you must decide if this is something so severe you need professional help or if it is something you can handle yourself.

To help make this decision, ask yourself three questions.

1. *Did something specific make me depressed?*

In other words, did you just have a big argument with your mate, your child, or one of your parents? Did you just flunk out of school or fail a test? Get laid off from your job or have someone you loved die? If something such as this recently happened, you probably have a good reason for being depressed particularly if this event *just* happened.

It's only reasonable and normal to be depressed if your best friend just died. However, if that person died a year ago and you're still depressed over it, this is not normal and may indicate you need professional help.

I knew a man who lost his teenage son in an automobile accident several years ago. Just prior to the accident the two of them had taken up wind surfing. The father looked forward to this because it was quality time spent together. Then his son was killed. After his death the father continued wind surfing with a fervor for several years as though this would somehow bring his son back. Of course it couldn't. The father realized that intellectually, but emotionally he just couldn't get over his son's death no matter how hard he tried. He even joined a therapy group composed of other parents who had lost a child. Such groups are specifically designed to help in these situations. This group helped a little, but it didn't eliminate the grief and remorse. Regardless of what he did or how much he tried he could not get over the loss of his son. This excessive grief reaction lasted for several years.

It's normal to grieve over a death. This grief reaction runs a fairly typical course from the initial shock and sorrow resulting from the loss to the recovery phase lasting anywhere from four to six weeks—to several years. During this grieving process, intense emotions of rage, anger, guilt, and anxiety are often present. Symptoms of depression frequently occur. This is why it is necessary to look at whether the depression is tied to something specific and logical, such as the death of a child.

2. Did you become depressed after some specific event took place or did the specific event just make your depression worse?

In other words, are you one of those people who has felt mildly depressed for some time? Most of the time you feel generally sad or blue and tend to tire much too easily. These symptoms are tolerable even though they're somewhat bothersome. When something bad happens to you, such as loosing your job, the symptoms get much worse. Now the blue feelings and fatigue are so bad you have difficulty working. All you want to do is sleep.

If this describes you, it suggests you are mildly depressed most of the time and this mild depression changes to a more severe level when something negative happens. If a mild level of depression exists most of the time, then you probably need to be concerned and do something about it.

A number of people have come to me stating their depression is due to the divorce they are going through or the trouble they are having with school, or—if they are a foreigner—their difficulty adjusting to a new culture. When I question them I ask about their symptoms prior to the divorce, the school problems, or the move. Many times I find they have battled some level of depression for years. This suggests it was not the event that caused the depression; rather, the present problem caused the symptoms of depression to become worse because of the additional stress in their life.

Studies of depression have revealed that it frequently becomes apparent after some period of stress such as having a baby, embarking on a crash diet, or going through a divorce. While these stressful events can bring on depression, they can also make an existing tendency worse. Therefore, it is necessary to determine if the symptoms of depression existed before the stressful event, although to a lesser degree.

If they are present prior to the stressful event, be prepared to do something about them. If they appeared only after the traumatic event, allow time for the stress to disappear. If the symptoms don't fade after the stressful event has been eliminated, do something about them!

Iva's case illustrates this point. Iva was a college graduate working as a manager in a print shop. Although she had been employed for only a few months she was given a great deal of responsibility for seeing that deadlines were met. This was enough stress for anyone, but it was something that went with the job and something she could handle. The problem was her boss, the owner of the print shop, was a tyrant. He demanded continual vigilance from her and would chastise her if she took off time for lunch or a break because she was not there to oversee the work. As a result, she was under continual pressure from his criticism as well as the deadlines of her job.

Her boss never had anything good to say about her work. He told her she was lazy and good-for-nothing. After several months of this abuse Iva became increasingly depressed. She decided she had to quit for her own sanity. She could not take it any longer and quit even though she did not have another job. Two months later Iva was still depressed, although now there was no reason for being depressed. Sure, she was unemployed, but she still had some money and she had lined up a number of interviews.

Because the depression did not lift Iva responded to one of my advertisements for research participants. Two weeks of treatment with the dietary program outlined in this book resulted in a lifting of her depression.

3. *Am I taking any medication that could cause my depression?*

There are numerous medications on the market that are miracle drugs and help keep us healthy and alive. While these drugs are beneficial, they do have some disadvantages. All drugs have the potential of producing side effects, one of which is depression. Medication used to control high blood pressure can produce depression in some individuals. Therefore, you must determine if the doldrums you're experiencing is possibly due to any medication you may be taking.

There are several ways to do this. The simplest and most direct is to ask your physician or the pharmacist that filled your prescription if depression is a potential side effect. Another technique is to look at your mood prior to, and after, taking the medication. If depression was not a problem before taking the medication, and it has been since, then the medication is a good candidate as the cause of the depression.

What Do You Do Now?

Let's assume you're feeling depressed or have many of the symptoms of depression and have asked yourself these three questions. Now you know the following:

A. You've had a number of the symptoms of depression for some time and these symptoms tend to get worse when you are under stress.

B. You know that you are not taking any medication that could be producing your symptoms of depression.

C. You know that either a specific event, such as the death of a loved one, did not cause the depression or—if there is a specific event, it just made the depression that was already there worse. You also know the specific event happened so long ago that it shouldn't still be causing you to be despondent.

D. You are concerned with the symptoms because you feel bad and want to feel better. This indicates you are depressed. You need to do something about it.

At this stage it would be helpful to get some idea of the severity of your depression as well as the type of depression you are experiencing. The American Psychiatric Association has published the *Diagnostic and Statistical Manual of Mental Disorders*, typically called DSM-III-R. This manual identifies the various types of depression, the symptoms representative of each type, and the severity of the depression. In the next chapter I will show you how you can use the information in this manual to get some idea of the severity of your depression and the type of depression you may be experiencing.

CHAPTER 14

Types of Depression

When Alice, a woman in her 50s, walked into my office she gave the appearance of a person who had been working all night trying to meet some deadline. Her hair looked like it had not been combed for several days, her clothes were wrinkled and mismatched, and she had no make-up on. This unruly appearance was apparently of no concern to her. She made no mention of it during the entire session.

As we talked I learned Alice had been in therapy on and off for several decades. She was currently seeing another therapist whose strategy was to try to get her to accept her condition because she was not getting any better; none of the previous therapy she had received had helped.

Alice was a bright, verbal woman working on her doctoral degree in architecture. As I continued asking questions, she told me that, at times, she had an abundance of energy. She would stay up all night studying for a test or working on a paper. She would get little sleep, but that didn't seem to matter because she had so much energy and got a lot of work accomplished. This was a time of great productivity for her; she felt good and was happy.

This exuberant feeling would not last though. After feeling so good and having so much energy for a while, she would feel herself coming down from this *high*. Gradually she become fatigued and depressed. During this time her productivity would come to a screeching halt and she could not perform academically at the level required of her. This was particularly distressing because she could not control when it occurred. If the feelings of depression came during exam time or when she had a paper to complete, her performance and grades suffered.

Classification of Mood Disorders

There are several different types of depression and many different ways of classifying them. Probably the most common classification system divides mood disorders into bipolar and unipolar disorders.

Bipolar Depression

Alice was experiencing a manic depressive disorder called *bipolar depression*. This is a disorder characterized by alternating between periods of depression and euphoria. Sometimes Alice would feel great and be on top of the world—constantly talking, socializing and needing very little sleep. Then she would cycle into a depression. she would feel terrible—have no motivation and always be tired.

A person with a bipolar disorder has drastic mood swings. Each one of these periods is distinct with identifiable characteristics. There is one distinct period during which the person's mood is extremely expansive and elevated. It is characterized by the individuals being unusually cheerful, having exceptional self-confidence, and feeling as though they are particularly knowledgeable or capable. During this period the person needs little sleep and has excessive energy. This excessive energy may result in their focusing on a specific activity such as a term paper, making friends, or buying clothes.

The other distinct period is characterized by depression. During this cycle they are down in the dumps and have no motivation or interest in doing anything. All they want to do is sleep or sit on a couch doing nothing. During this period food may not be appealing or they may be very irritable and moody. Although Alice's behavior was not as excessive as that exhibited by some with a bipolar disorder, she exhibited many of the characteristics.

Bipolar depression is a very serious disorder and extremely distressing to those who suffer from it. Unfortunately, it doesn't seem to be responsive to the treatment program discussed in this book. Therefore, I will not focus any more attention on this disorder. Instead, let's talk about another type of mood disorder called *unipolar depression*. It is the type of mood disorder that affects most people.

Unipolar Depression

Unipolar depression, as its name indicates, is the type of depression where a person becomes down and stays down. There is no alternating between cycles. There is only one direction that the mood disturbance takes: in the direction of depression.

When this type of depression develops it's as though the individual has fallen into a deep dark hole and cannot get out. Initiative and motivation almost cease and the desire to do anything declines to nil. This is the way just about everyone with unipolar depression feels, particularly if the depression is severe.

Types of Unipolar Depression

The *Diagnostic and Statistical Manual of Mental Disorders* classifies unipolar depression as major depression or dysthymia.

Major Depression

Major depression is the more serious of the unipolar mood disorders and accounts for the majority of cases. The characteristics that distinguish it follow:

1. A depressed mood or a loss of interest or pleasure in all, or almost all activities.
2. Appetite change (either an increase or a decrease).
3. Weight change (either gaining or losing weight).

4. Psychomotor agitation or retardation (Always moving around or moving and talking slower than normal).
5. Fatigue or energy loss.
6. Feelings of worthlessness, or excessive or inappropriate guilt.
7. Difficulty thinking or concentrating.
8. Recurrent thoughts of death, suicide, or attempts of suicide.

Each characteristic is important. However, some are more important than others and you do not have to have all of them to have major depression.

The first characteristic is the most important and the one you *must* have to have major depression. If you do not, then you can be sure you don't have major depression.

Even if you do have the first characteristic and feel depressed or as though you have lost interest in almost all activities, you still may not have major depression. This feeling must have lasted at least two weeks and you must have had at least four of the other characteristics for at least two weeks to qualify as having major depression.

As you can see, making a diagnosis of major depression isn't easy. It is further complicated by the fact that you must rule out the possibility that the symptoms you have may be caused by some physical illness, medication you may be taking, plus alcoholism or drug abuse. It is also important to eliminate the possibility that the depression is caused by a reaction to the loss of a loved one.

Probably the best way to identify whether you may be suffering from major depression is to answer the following questions:

1. Have you felt depressed, sad, hopeless, discouraged, *down in the dumps* or something similar most of the day, nearly every day for the past two weeks?
____Yes ____No

2. Have you had a decreased interest or pleasure in all, or almost all, activities most of the day, nearly every day for the past two weeks? In other words, have you

she no longer felt the inner tension and agitation that kept her from being able to sit still.

Does the slowing down or the agitation I just described fit you? ____Yes ____No

6. Do you feel fatigued or like you have no energy? Have you had this feeling nearly every day for the last two weeks?

Loss of energy is one of the hallmarks of depression. Most depressed individuals experience a decrease in energy level and constant fatigue even though they have done nothing exhausting. They may have even been lying in bed sleeping most of the day and still feel fatigued. Many times this fatigue makes the person feel as though even the smallest task is difficult or impossible to accomplish. Lucy Freeman, in her book *Cry for Love* cites a case of a depressed person who felt even brushing his teeth was a monumental task.

Do you feel tired all the time regardless of how much sleep you get? ____Yes ____No

7. Do you feel worthlessness or guilty and have you felt this way every day for the last two weeks?

A person who is depressed will have feelings that vary from feeling very inadequate to feeling totally worthless. This worthless feeling is most apparent when the depressed person fails at something, even if it is as insignificant as spilling milk on the floor. When something like this happens it makes them feel as though they can't do anything right. Over time, the depression and the sense of failure can create excessive guilt.

Nancy, the teacher we met earlier, portrays this very accurately. Over several years she became more and more depressed. When I saw her the first time she felt very guilty about not being a good mother, wife, and teacher because she did not have the energy to fix meals, do the laundry, or prepare for class.

Do you have similar feelings of worthlessness or guilt? ____Yes ____No

8. Has your ability to think or concentrate diminished or do you find it difficult to make decisions nearly every day?

   A depressed person has difficulty concentrating. Their thinking slows down and their decision making ability is reduced. For example, Nancy claimed that she could not make even the smallest decision because she was afraid she would be wrong. It is also common for a depressed person to feel as though their memory is very poor or that they can't remember as well as they used to.

   Do you have trouble making decisions or do you have difficulty concentrating?   ____Yes ____No

9. Do you think about dying or about committing suicide?

   It is very common for a depressed person to wish they were dead—to contemplate suicide. Frequently, they think everyone around them would be better off if they were dead. Most of the time these thoughts occur without any plan to commit suicide, and even if they did, a depressed person frequently states they couldn't carry out any plan they may have thought of. Sometimes they do, however. These thoughts are serious and should never be taken lightly.

   If you have had any such thoughts and they continue day after day, please get immediate help for your depression. You can try the dietary intervention outlined in this book; it works wonders for some people. But if it doesn't work for you, seek immediate help from a mental health professional.

   The significant issue is, "Do you have thoughts of dying or committing suicide?"   ____Yes ____No

At this point I have given you nine symptoms of major depression. If you have answered yes to five of these nine symptoms, and *at least one of the five* is either the first or second symptom, and the five symptoms have *all* been present during the past two weeks, then you are probably experiencing a major depressive episode.

As I stated earlier, answering these nine questions will only give you an *indication* of whether you are experiencing a major depressive episode. A mental health professional is necessary to make the final diagnosis and rule out such factors as an organic cause. However, if you meet the criteria based on the above questions, you should seriously consider getting treatment. You can start by trying the dietary treatment. It is fast acting, simple to self-administer, and has been proven to be successful in treating many, but not all depressed individuals.

If, based on your answers to the above nine questions, you do not meet the criteria for major depression, celebrate. However, this does not mean that you are not depressed. You could be experiencing a less serious form of depression which is called dysthymia.

Dysthymia

A person with Dysthymia is someone who has suffered from a mild degree of depression for many years. The best way to determine if you may be suffering from dysthymia is to answer the following questions.

1. During the past two years have you been bothered by depression most of the day, more days than not? In other words, during the past two years, have you felt depressed or *down in the dumps* most of the day, more days than not. ____Yes ____No

If your answer to this question is no, then you are probably not suffering from dysthymia. If your answer is yes, however, then you may be depending on your responses to the following questions.

2. When you are feeling low or depressed, does your appetite change? Do you loose your appetite or start overeating? ____Yes ____No

3. When you are feeling depressed, do you have trouble sleeping or do you sleep too much? ____Yes ____No

4. When you are feeling depressed, do you have little energy to do things or do you feel fatigued and tired a lot? ____Yes ____No

5. When you are feeling depressed, do you feel worthless, like you are a failure? Are you down on yourself and have feelings of low self-esteem?   ____Yes ____No

6. When you are feeling depressed, do you have trouble concentrating or making decisions?   ____Yes ____No

7. When you are feeling depressed do you feel pessimistic about the future? ____Yes ____No

If your answer to question 1 is yes and your answer to two of the other six questions is yes you may have dysthymia. Now you need to go back to the questions you answered *yes* and ask yourself the following question: Has there ever been a two month period of time during the last two years when you were never without these symptoms? If your answer to this question is no, then you may be suffering from dysthymia.

Remember that the answers to these questions only represent a suggestion that you may have dysthymia. There are other factors that must be taken into consideration in making an accurate diagnosis. But if your answers indicate that you do have dysthymia, consider this a real possibility and consider obtaining treatment. This could be the dietary treatment presented in this book.

Depression Not Meeting The Criteria
for Dysthymia or Major Depression

Now let's assume you have not met the criteria for either major depression or dysthymia. This suggests you do not have either of these two categories of mood disorder. It does not mean you are not depressed and do not need some help. Remember that to meet the criteria for dysthymia you must have felt depressed more days than not for the past two years. Many people feel depressed and have symptoms such as a loss of appetite, fatigue, confusion, and insomnia and attempt to get help in eliminating these symptoms immediately, rather than tolerate them for two years as would be required for a diagnosis of dysthymia.

John is a good example of such an individual. When I first saw John he was complaining of being tired, moody, and generally lethargic for months. These feeling started occurring about nine months earlier when he made a decision to go to graduate school at a university located in another state. When he informed his fiancee of this decision, she refused to go with him and broke off the engagement. Shortly after their break-up John started feeling depressed.

John attributed the depression, fatigue, and moodiness he was experiencing to not having gotten over losing his fiancee. However, John couldn't shake the blues and the constant depression. It wasn't so bad that he couldn't function, yet John just didn't feel well and was constantly *down.*

Because the depression lasted so long and he couldn't seem to shake it, he needed help. Fortunately, John sought assistance. Within two weeks after changing his diet, his depression, blue feelings, moodiness, and fatigue were gone.

Now that you have read this chapter and have answered the questions, what is your diagnosis? Are you experiencing a major depressive episode, dysthymia, or are you just experiencing a continuing level of mild depression that you can't seem to get over? If any of these three situations exist, you need some help.

CHAPTER 15

Take Control of Your Life

All of us want to feel good and enjoy a healthy and happy life. No one wants to be saddled with the misery of depression. In this book I have presented a simple dietary change that you can use to possibly eliminate your depression. This is the beauty of the diet. You don't need anyone to prescribe a medicine or help you change your life style or your thought patterns. You can do it yourself and control your own destiny.

At several points in the book I have emphasized that everyone's depression will not be eliminated by eating a refined sugar and caffeine-free diet. This is why I have provided, in chapter 6, a list of questions you can answer to determine if your depression may be due to diet. If your answer to these questions indicates that your despondence is due to diet, then you can take control of your life and possibly eliminate the despair you are feeling. All you need is to develop the attitude and resolve that you can do it and then start changing your diet.

I know that depression can make you feel very tired and even small changes seem like monumental tasks. These are the feelings that create pessimism and make you think nothing will turn out right—that you don't have the ability to eliminate your depression. But you do. The first step is to believe in yourself. Start thinking, "I can do it. All I have to do is change my diet. All I have to do is eliminate refined sugar and caffeine and I can feel good again."

I know changing your thoughts from negative to positive can be difficult when you are feeling depressed. But having positive thoughts will help you get started on the dietary change. Remember the case of Nancy I presented in chapter 5. It took her two weeks to decide how she would arrange for the care of her small child so she could come to the psychology clinic. This is a classic example of how negative thoughts can inhibit action. Nancy's thoughts focused on "How she would get to the clinic and who would care for her child." She did not take that additional step which involved coming up with a list of people who could take care of her child or coming up with a schedule so that she could have access to the family car. It was difficult for her to get past thinking how difficult it was going to be or how much energy it was going to take to make the necessary arrangements.

In chapter 8, I told you about a letter I received from a woman who was very depressed and so obsessed with losing weight that she starved herself. In this letter she asked for my help. I wrote her a rather lengthy response instructing her to forget about losing weight until she had her depression under control. I also informed her that her depression may be due to diet. I inclosed my diet with instructions to follow it closely for at least two weeks to see if it would get rid of those low feelings she was having.

About six months later I received another letter from this woman. Her first sentence stated "I am on the come back trail!" She took my advice and followed the diet, particularly eliminating caffeine. If she consumes caffeine she says that she gets headaches and it puts her in a bad mood. Not only did the depression disappear when she changed her diet, but her self confidence was returning. She now has plans to go back to school this fall and work toward a degree in physical therapy.

Here is a person that was ready to drive off an embankment to end her life prior to changing her diet.

However, she took control of her life and decided to change her diet to see if it would do any good. This is exactly what you need to do. You can be the master of your own destiny.

Some of the individuals I have worked with have difficulty believing that the amount of sugar or caffeine in their diet could be causing their depression. They don't consume much of either substance, or at least they don't think they do. They also eat a rather good diet. If you are experiencing depression, don't be fooled by this. Some people are very sensitive to either caffeine and/or sugar and it takes very little to maintain their depression. The Appendix presents the diets of several of the individuals who have participated in my studies and who experienced a lift from the diet. These sample diets reflect the variability in the type of meals eaten by such individuals. If you will look at these sample diets, I think you can see that the first one might fit many people. You can also see that there is not a lot of sugar or caffeine included in it. Yet this person's depression improved when following the caffeine and sugar-free diet. This is the point I want to make. Don't assume that the diet can't help you just because you don't consume much sugar or caffeine. If you are experiencing depression and everything you have read in this book indicates that the diet will help you—try it. You might be pleasantly surprised.

APPENDIX

Food Record
for One Dietary Responder

Day 1

Breakfast

Two cups coffee with cream and sugar
Two pieces of toast with butter
12 ounce glass of grapefruit juice
Two pieces of bacon

Lunch

Fried catfish
Baked potato with chives, cheese and butter
Salad with ranch dressing
Half a biscuit
Two glasses of ice tea

Before Dinner

Half a can of beer
Rum and coke

Dinner

Two glasses of wine

Egg drop soup
Caesar's salad
Baked red snapper
Asparagus
Carrot cake
Cup coffee with cream and sugar

After Dinner

Club soda

Day 2

Breakfast

Fried egg
Bacon
Biscuit
6 ounce glass of grapefruit juice
Two cups of coffee with cream and sugar

Lunch

Cheese sandwich
12 ounce glass grapefruit juice
Hand full of potato chips
One raw asparagus spear

Dinner

Half bottle of beer
12 ounce glass club soda with lemon
Two raw asparagus spears
Doritoes with picadillo sauce
Two bite size butterfingers
Dr. Pepper

Day 3

Breakfast

One cup coffee with cream and sugar

Lunch

Hamburger with fries
Coke
Potato chips—small bag
Handful of honey roasted peanuts

Dinner

Bottle of beer
Glass of ice tea
Four ounce broiled steak
Baked potato with butter, sour cream and bacon bits
Salad with blue cheese dressing
Three chocolate chip cookies

Food Record
for a Second Dietary Responder

Day 1

Breakfast

Cinnamon and raisin bagel with cream cheese
One 8 ounce glass of milk
Two cups of tea

Mid-Morning

Cup of coffee
Diet coke

Lunch

Cheeseburger
French fries
Hot chocolate

After Work

One bottle of beer
Snickers bar

Dinner

Large taco

Day 2

Breakfast

Cup hot tea with milk
Two chocolate chip cookies
Two eggs
Four slices of bread

Lunch

Two ounces pork and beans

Peanut butter and jelly sandwich
Three glasses of ice tea

Dinner

Large catfish
Salad—lettuce, tomato, and avocado
Two 6 ounce glasses of Chablis wine

After Dinner

Six ounces of beer

Day 3

Breakfast

One 8 ounce can of Dr. Pepper
Snickers bar
Four chocolate chip cookies

Lunch

Bowl of vegetable and beef soup
Two slices of bread with cheese
Four glasses of tea

Dinner

Bean and beef burrito with cheese
Apple
Cup of coffee

Bibliography

Anderson, R.A., Polansky, M.M., Bryden, N.A., et al. (1982). Urinary chromium excretion of human subjects: Effects of chromium supplementation and glucose loading. *American Journal of Clinical Nutrition, 36*, 1184-1193.

Baldessarini, R.J. (1984). Treatment of depression by altering monamine metabolism: Precursors and metabolic inhibitor. *Psychopharmacology Bulletin, 20*, 224-239.

Beck, A.T. (1972). *Depression: Causes and Treatment.* Philadelphia: University of Pennsylvania Press.

Brezinova, V. (1974). Effect of caffeine on sleep: EEG study in late middle age people. *British Journal of Clinical Pharmacology, 1*, 203-208.

Charney, D.S., Heninger, G.R., & Jatlow, P.I. (1985). Increased anxiogenic effects of caffeine in panic disorders. *Archives of General Psychiatry, 42*, 233-243.

Christensen, L., Krietsch, K., White, B. & Stagner, B. (1985). The impact of a dietary change on emotional disturbance. *Journal of Abnormal Psychology, 94*, 565-579.

Christensen, L., Krietsch, K. & White, B. (1989). Development, cross-validation, and assessment of reliability of the Christensen Dietary Distress Inventory. *Canadian Journal of Behavioral Science, 21*, 1-15.

Christensen, L. & Burrows, R. (1990). Dietary treatment of depression. *Behavior Therapy, 21*, 183-193.

Curb, J.D., Reed, D.M., Kautz, J.A., & Yano, K. (1986). Coffee, caffeine, and serum cholesterol in Japanese men in Hawaii. *American Journal of Epidemiology, 123*, 648-655

Fernstrom, M.H., Krowinski, R.L. & Kupfer, D.J. (1987). Appetite and food preference in depression: Effects of imipramine treatment. *Biological Psychiatry, 22*, 529-539.

Fernstrom, J.D. & Faller, G.V. (1978). Neutral amino acids in the brain: Changes in response to food ingestion. *Journal of Neurochemistry, 30*, 1531-1538.

Gelenberg, A.J., Gibson, C.J. & Wojcik, J.D. (1982). Neurotransmitter precursors for the treatment of depression. *Psychopharmacology Bulletin, 18*, 7-8.

Georgotas, A. & Cancro, R. (eds.). (1988). *Depression and Mania*. New York: Elsevier.

Goldberg, M.R., Curatolo, P.W., Tung, C.S. & Robertson, D. (1982). Caffeine down-regulates beta adrenoreceptors in rat forebrain. *Neuroscience Letters, 31*, 47-52.

Goldstein, A., & Kaizer, S. (1969). Psychotropic effects of caffeine in man. III. A questionnaire survey of coffee drinking and its effects in a group of housewives. *Clinical Pharmacology and Therapeutics, 10*, 477-490.

Goldstein, A., Warren, R., & Kaizer, S. (1965). Psychotropic effects of caffeine in man. I. Individual differences in sensitivity to caffeine-induced wakefulness. *Journal of Pharmacology and Experimental Therapeutics, 149*, 156-160.

Greden, J.F., Fontaine, P., Lubetsky, M. & Chamberlin, K. (1978). Anxiety and depression associated with caffeinism among psychiatric inmates. *American Journal of Psychiatry, 13*, 963-966.

Growdon, J.H. & Wurtman, R.J. (1979). Dietary influences on the synthesis of neurotransmitters in the brain. *Nutrition Reviews, 37*, 129-136.

James, J.E., Stirling, K.P., & Hampton B.A.M. (1985). Caffeine fading: Behavioral treatment of caffeine abuse. *Behavior Therapy, 16*, 15-27.

Krietsch, K., Christensen, L., & White, B. (1988). Prevalence, presenting symptoms, and psychological characteristics of individuals experiencing a diet-related mood-disturbance. *Behavior Therapy, 19*, 593-604.

LaCroix, A.Z., Mead, L.A., Liang, K., Thomas, C.B., & Pearson, T.A. (1986). Coffee consumption and the incidence of coronary heart disease. *New England Journal of Medicine, 315*, 977-982.

Levinson, W., & Dunn, P.M. (1986). Nonassociation of caffeine and fibrocystic breast disease. *Archives of Internal Medicine, 146*, 1773-1775.

Lieberman, H.R., Caballero, B. & Finer, N. (1986). The composition of lunch determines afternoon plasma tryptophan ratios in humans. *Journal of Neural Transmission, 65*, 211-217.

Shen, W.W., & D'Souza, T.C. (1979). Cola-induced psychotic organic brain syndrome. *Rocky Mountain Medical Journal*, 312-313.

Spring, B., Chiodo, J., & Bowen, D.J. (1987). Carbohydrates, tryptophan, and behavior: A methodological review. *Psychological Bulletin, 102*, 234-256.

Veleber, D.M. & Templer, D.I. (1984). Effects of caffeine on anxiety and depression. *Journal of Abnormal Psychology, 93*, 120-122.

Wurtman, R.J., Hefti, J., & Melamed, E. (1980). Precursor control of neurotransmitter synthesis. *Pharmacology Reviews, 32*, 315-355.

Index

Give the Gift of Happiness
to Your Depressed
Friends and Loved Ones!

ORDER FORM

YES, I want _____ copies of *The Food-Mood Connection* at $9.95 each, plus $2 shipping per book. (Texas residents please include $.74 in state sales tax.) Canadian orders must be accompanied by a postal money order in U.S. funds. Allow 30 days for delivery.

☐ Check/MO order enclosed ● Charge my ☐ VISA ☐ MC

Name _____ Phone _____

Address _____

City/State/Zip _____

Card # _____ Expires_____

Signature _____

*Check your leading bookstore or call
your credit card order to (800) 637-6459*

Please make your check payable and return to:

Pro-Health Publications
P.O. Box 682
College Station, TX 77841